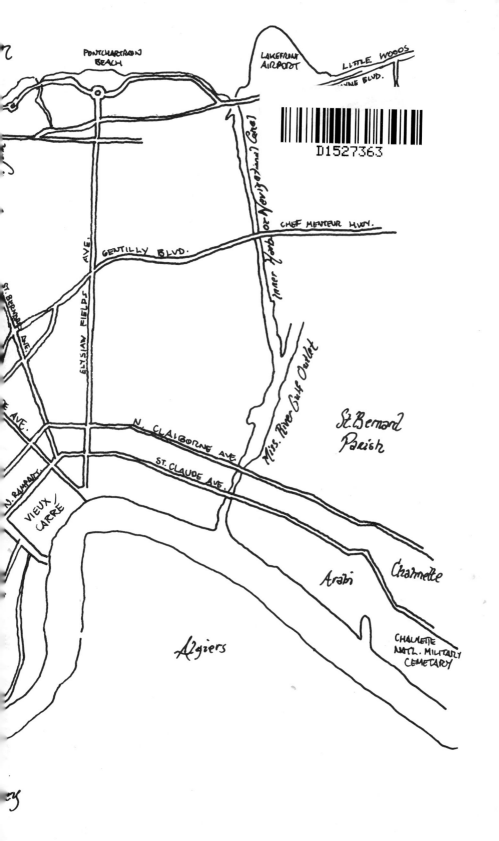

Uptown Downtown

ENDPAPER MAP EXPLANATION

The endpaper map will orient readers to the street plan of New Orleans and especially to the Uptown and Downtown sections where we grew up. First find Canal Street, the dividing line between the two sections. The area below or south (loosely speaking) of Canal Street is Uptown and the area above or north (loosely speaking) of Canal is Downtown. Actually the street designations north and south have limited significance because of the city's location within a bend (Bienville's *beau croissant*---beautiful crescent) of the Mississippi River, between the river and Lake Pontchartrain to the north. Direction by compass is a hopeless task in New Orleans because our points of reference are not the usual north, south, east, and west but rather riverside, lakeside, uptown, and downtown. While Canal Street is the point of orientation for streets designated north and south, many major "north" and "south" streets follow the bend in the river and actually for part of their route run east or west. North and South Claiborne avenues illustrate this dramatically.

So when in New Orleans, do as the natives---find your way around by travelling uptown, downtown, riverside, and lakeside. If you'd like to meet us at the Pontchartrain Hotel, it's uptown on the downtown, lakeside corner of St. Charles Avenue and Josephine Street.

Uptown/Downtown
Growing Up in New Orleans

Elsie Martinez and Margaret LeCorgne

Introduction By Charles L. Dufour

Illustrations by Meg Barker

The Center for Louisiana Studies
University of Southwestern Louisiana
Lafayette, Louisiana

The Center for Louisiana Studies
The University of Southwestern Louisiana
Lafayette, La. 70504

©1986 by The University of Southwestern Louisiana
Published 1986.
Printed in the United States of America
92 91 90 89 88 87   5 4 3 2 1

Library of Congress Catalog Number: 86-71547
ISBN Number: 0-940984-32-6

To: Johnny
To: Margaret Marie and Robert

CONTENTS

Foreword

In New Orleans no one believes in the compass.

Directions in most American cities are standardized to conform to the magnetic needle: North, South, East, West.

But not in New Orleans.

To be sure, streets that cross Canal Street with the same name are designated North and South This or That, but only as a convenient device to indicate "below" or "above" Canal Street.

New Orleans' mistrust in the compass is best exemplified in the city's longest street, Claiborne Avenue, which runs from city boundary to city boundary. North Claiborne generally runs Southeast, while South Claiborne generally runs Northwest.

Why? Because the oft-bending Mississippi River has discredited the compass. The river, which is the reason New Orleans was founded, the reason New Orleans exists, determines direction in the Crescent City. Replacing the points of the compass are the designations: Uptown, Downtown, River, Lake.

Uptown includes the area up-river from Canal Street; Downtown embraces the area down-river from Canal Street. Each of these sections of New Orleans, while sharing many things in common, has a lifestyle of its own---folklore and folkways, customs and traditions which differ in detail, if not in principle.

Nostalgia is an enchanted Childland. It is ever inviting grown-ups to turn back the clock and ramble happily down the exciting lanes of Memory. That is what Margaret LeCorgne and Elsie Martinez, native Orleanians, have done delightfully in their *Uptown-Downtown: Growing Up in New Orleans*.

One of the authors, Mrs. Martinez, grew up in Downtown New Orleans; the other, Mrs. LeCorgne, grew up in Uptown New Orleans. Together, they have recaptured the New Orleans of their childhood and youth, New Orleans of the 1930s and 40s, as young people half a century ago enjoyed it with delight. Their collaboration was the result of their realization that "growing up in New Orleans was different from growing up anywhere else in the United States---or in the world, for that matter." This difference was, over the decades, brought home to them when they met people "who had never heard of a King Cake, or a nectar soda, had never visited a St. Joseph altar or gone to a jazz funeral, didn't know how to eat a boiled crab and looked bewildered when we mentioned the neutral ground . . . or lagniappe . . . or the banquette."

The authors decided to depict New Orleans, not in a unified narrative, but in a series of vignettes and reminiscences, each author contributing alternating sketches of Uptown and Downtown New Orleans. Their style, I should say their styles, are lively and their memories are sharp. The result is a charming picture of New Orleans as children and young adults experienced it four and five decades ago.

The reader will get the feel of these two sections of New Orleans as Uptown and Downtown were half a century ago. He will be introduced to neighborhoods, neighbors, shops, and recreation areas; to schools, private and public; shopping expeditions and shopping habits; going to the movies or "getting culture;" holy days and holidays; summer and winter games; excursions to Canal Street, the lake, the parks, the French Quarter; and, of course, Carnival and Mardi Gras itself.

The rich memories of these two accomplished writers will stir the memories of an Orleanian of mature years and reveal to young people and non-Orleanians the enduring charm of the city Bienville founded 268 years ago.

Charles L. Dufour

Prologue

A few years ago a friend of ours who grew up in the Midwest gave a birthday party for her ten-year-old son. She did what a lot of parents do in New Orleans---she rented the St. Charles Avenue streetcar and fifty children enjoyed ice cream and cake while rocking up and down the city's most prestigious avenue. The "child" who enjoyed it most, however, was our friend who never lost her smile despite the pandemonium of fifty youngsters popping balloons and playing spaceship on a lurching, rattling streetcar. "Isn't this fun?!" she exclaimed in wonder. "Where else could kids do something like this on their birthday? Boy, they are so lucky to be growing up in New Orleans."

That was probably the first time we, the co-authors, both of us native New Orleanians, realized fully that growing up in New Orleans was different from growing up anywhere else in the United States---or in the world, for that matter. We had noticed *something* was different, of course, whenever we'd met people who had never heard of a King Cake or a nectar soda, had never visited a St. Joseph Altar or seen a jazz funeral, didn't know how to eat a boiled crab and looked bewildered when we mentioned the neutral ground (street median), or lagniappe (a little something extra) or the banquette (sidewalk).

We were further struck by the difference New Orleans makes when a neighbor of ours told us with some amusement of taking her young grandson to Pittsburgh to visit relatives and while there attending a Columbus Day parade. The youngster was excited about going to a parade and as the first float approached them he began jumping up and down and shouting, "Throw me something, Mister," just as he always does at Mardi Gras parades in New Orleans, where maskers shower paradegoers with favors, commonly called "throws." The little boy gradually realized that the men on the parade floats were not throwing any beads or doubloons or trinkets; they weren't throwing anything at all. They were just smiling and waving at everyone. Crestfallen, he exclaimed in disgust, "They call *this* a parade?" and lost all interest in the colorful, but un-carnival-like Pittsburgh procession.

Most American cities have some unique qualities that make growing up in that particular place different from growing up anywhere else, but it's unlikely that any of them are quite so singular as New Orleans. Because it was a French and Spanish city for eighty-five years before becoming a part of the United States, its character and culture were stamped in the southern European mold. It was Latin, Mediterranean, Catholic---but with a Creole accent that gave it individuality. Americans who poured into the city after the Louisiana Purchase of 1803 felt like they were in a foreign country. Americans who come here today are still struck by the European quality of New Orleans, and we've met Europeans who say it reminds them of home.

We were discussing all of this one day and agreed that when we were growing up we didn't know or care much about the history of the city or think about why we celebrated Mardi Gras, King Cake Day, All Saints' Day and St. Joseph's Day, or why New Orleans was known as "the city that care forgot." Those things were all just part of the fabric of our lives and we accepted and enjoyed them without question. In comparing notes about our growing-up years we discovered that while we shared the same unique culture and customs of New Orleans, we often experienced them differently. One of us had an "uptown" experience and the other had a "downtown" experience. We don't think either of us at the time was aware of the "mystique" of Uptown New Orleans or of the historical and cultural background of Downtown New Orleans. They were just the areas in which we lived and Canal Street was the dividing line between them. When one of us went to Canal Street she was going "uptown" and when the other went to Canal Street she was going "downtown."

We thought it would be fun to share our experiences with others, so we've put together these vignettes of growing up in New Orleans, uptown and downtown. Of course growing up in the 1980s in New Orleans isn't at all the same experience as growing up when we did. For one thing the city looked a lot different in the thirties and forties. The tallest building was the 23-story Hibernia Bank Building with its classic Greek-style cupola. There were no shopping malls. We did all our retail shopping on and around Canal Street. We bought our groceries and other day-to-day necessities at little stores within walking distance of our homes. We were surrounded by water. Besides the Mississippi River and Lake Pontchartrain, we had bayous, canals, lagoons, and open gutters often filled with rainwater. The city was crisscrossed with bridges and railroad tracks instead of overpasses and underpasses and we lived routinely with bridges being up and railroad barricades being down as we traveled around town. Despite these obstacles, get around we did, often with the help of a public transportation system that was probably one of the best in the country. For seven cents we could go from uptown to downtown, to the Lakefront, the outlying sections of Metairie and Gentilly and for a few more pennies, we could even cross the river on the ferry to Algiers. The river was not nearly so visible or accessible then as it is today. As a port city, New Orleans draws its lifeblood from the Mississippi---indeed the river is the city's reason for existence---but it was not an important part of our growing-up experiences, except for an occasional ferry ride. We learned a lot more about the Mississippi from reading Mark Twain than we ever did from seeing it in our backyard.

Lake Pontchartrain, on the other hand, was familiar to everyone. A favorite amusement area, its shores were a place for picnicking, fishing, shrimping, crabbing, sunbathing, and swimming. The beautification wrought by the Works Progress Administration during the Depression made the winding drive around the Lake from West End at the western border of the city to Little Woods several miles to the east, a scenic delight. Of course New Orleans East was a swamp and Park Island in Bayou St. John, now one of the city's most expensive pieces of real estate, was a favorite dove hunting area. The Bayou was crowded with houseboats and the New Basin Canal, site of today's Pontchartrain Expressway, was a bustling waterway filled with barges, fishing boats, and pleasure craft.

Our neighborhoods were busy with street vendors hawking everything from figs to clothes poles (long forked branches made to hold up clothes lines) and our front porches were extended living rooms. We lived without the luxury of air-conditioning or the fascination of television. Rather, our lives were sparked by the ubiquitous presence of radio and the almost mesmerizing magic of the movies.

We were a stable community. It was rare, and somewhat exciting, to meet anyone who was not a native New Orleanian. It was even rarer for a New Orleanian to abandon the city of his birth and move elsewhere.

Racially, New Orleans was then a predominantly white community. Almost seventy percent of its citizens were white and thirty per cent were black. Demographically, it was the most integrated city in the United States with blacks and whites living in close proximity in almost every residential area of the city. That was as far as integration went, however, for educational as well as all other public and private institutions and facilities were strictly segregated.

Our growing-up years spanned two devastating epochs---the Great Depression and World War II, both of which brought dramatic changes to the city. The lean Depression years meant hard times for most New Orleanians and had even tragic consequences for those who lost not only their jobs but their homes, investments---everything they had. The times instilled a continuing habit of thriftiness in many of us and a careful attitude about spending and saving which is rare in today's throw-away society.

The Depression also brought unexpected bounty to New Orleans and did a great deal to change the appearance of the city. The expenditure of federal funds on public projects throughout New Orleans served to upgrade and beautify buildings, parks, playgrounds, and other recreational facilities. Such funding also provided employment for artists and writers, enriching the city's cultural life as well.

Public works gave way to military activity as the city mobilized following the outbreak of World War II. New Orleans' strategic location near the mouth of the Mississippi and the Gulf of Mexico and its importance as a port facility made it one of the country's prime military centers. We soon got used to seeing soldiers and sailors strolling along Canal Street but we never got used to rumors of Nazi submarines lurking at the mouth of the river, poised to attack the city.

The war years were time out as far as city projects or development were concerned. But the years immediately following the war saw an astonishing change. New Orleans shed its provincial, backwater image as it experienced a surge of building and modernization. Diversity and mobility became a part of New Orleans life. Despite these changes, the city's mood and character have remained surprisingly the same. The famous architect Benjamin Latrobe, on a visit to the city in 1819, admired the architecture and French character of the city but lamented that "in a few years this will be an American town." He couldn't have been further off the mark. One hundred and sixty-seven years later it is still not "an American town"---in the sense that most towns in the United States are. In spite of the visible and invisible changes that have occurred since World War II, and the extension of the city to the east and over the river, it remains at heart a Latin Mediterranean enclave in the midst of the American South. There is no mistaking New Orleans for any other place in the United States. The Creole stamp still remains and the laid-back, laissez-faire attitude still dominates.

There is still the New Orleans penchant for "making a connection." The city has retained a surprisingly small-town atmosphere, a place where any new acquaintance may turn out to be a distant relative or at least a friend of a relative. You still hear people say things like "and who was your mother?" It sounds snobbish but is usually said simply to try to trace a connection. People are always saying "it's a small world, isn't it?" While few New Orleanians meet these days under the clock at D. H. Holmes department store (a longtime tradition), it's surprising how often you'll bump into someone you know if you turn up there on any given day.

It seems "the more things change, the more they stay the same," for in spite of all the superficial changes in the city, its fundamental values and way of life continue. As we've watched our children and their friends grow up, we've seen them celebrate Mardi Gras and All Saints' Day, take delight in King Cakes and summer snowballs, enjoy sailing and fishing on Lake Pontchartrain and picnicking in Audubon Park and City Park, and thrill to the excitement of Sugar Bowl football games—whether in the old Tulane Stadium or the Superdome.

But we are sorry they never had a chance to savor a childhood marked by the special delights of the front porch or the fireplace; or experience a streetcar ride on West End Boulevard along the New Basin Canal; or laugh at the amateur performances on Professor Schramm's radio show, or enjoy a nectar soda at the corner drugstore or a slice of ice cold watermelon at a neighborhood stand; or marvel at the wonders of the seafood stalls at the French Market. While bridges and interstates have made once "faraway" places like Algiers and Eastern New Orleans just minutes away from central New Orleans, other areas have become inaccessible or invisible. It's no longer possible to enjoy an uninterrupted drive along the shores of Lake Pontchartrain, the colorful camps (houses on stilts) at Little Woods on the Lake's eastern shore are hidden by a cement levee, and many familiar landmarks like the St. Charles Hotel and the New Orleans Public Library at Lee Circle have disappeared from the scene.

But our children have experienced the indefinable spirit of New Orleans, a spirit marked by a readiness for and anticipation of celebration. We always seem to be celebrating something or getting ready to celebrate something.

A friend of ours* told us of an incident we think typifies this spirit. One Easter shortly before World War II, the late Archbishop Joseph Francis Rum-

*Florence Henderson, founder and manager of the Catholic Bookstore, New Orleans.

mel was getting ready to celebrate Mass at St. Louis Cathedral in the French Quarter---with all the pomp and circumstance that was current with the Catholic Church in those days. A crowd assembled outside the church and a man held up his four-year-old daughter on his shoulders so she could see the archbishop and his entourage as they proceeded from the cathedral alley to the church. First came acolytes with candles, then thurifers (incense bearers), followed by seminarians and priests, then the Knights of St. Gregory with tall plumed hats, and finally the archbishop dressed in the grand regalia of his office---white robes, red cloak and ermine cape, jeweled miter, staff and satin slippers. As he passed the little girl, she clapped her hands and began shouting "Throw me something, Mister, throw me something." Everyone, including the archbishop, entered the church laughing. Only in New Orleans.

We hope that the following vignettes and reminiscenses will give our readers a taste of what it was like to grow up in a New Orleans that seems very different from the city we know today---and yet, as you will see, in some ways very much the same.

Uptown Downtown

Downtown--
Where New Orleans Was Born

At a very early age I became aware that there was a vast difference between uptown New Orleans and downtown New Orleans. Of course they differed geographically. Uptown lay on the south side of Canal Street, the city's major thoroughfare, and downtown lay on the north side of Canal Street. However, the real difference between them was less tangible but more powerful than physical separation.

Except for the French Quarter, downtown had no aura of romance or mystery. It was just plain downtown---ordinary, rather pedestrian, nondescript. At least it seemed so to me. But *uptown*---the word conveyed class, desirability. The difference between uptown and downtown is humorously pinpointed in a story told by the late newspaperman Howard Jacobs. It concerns a colored maid who worked several years for an uptown matron. The maid moved downtown and went to work for a family in the Seventh Ward. Instructing her new maid, the downtown matron cautioned her when using a new can of household cleanser to punch out only two holes in the can. The maid looked at her new employer with some disdain and replied: "Uptown, we punches out all the holes."

I experienced the power of the uptown reputation when I was in the seventh grade. I was sadly disappointed when one of my best friends moved from our neighborhood to an uptown neighborhood. We were disconsolate at being parted (it was as though she were moving to New York) but she appeared to be consoled by the fact that she would be going to an uptown high school, Eleanor McMain on South Claiborne Avenue and Joseph Street (In those Depression days there was no eighth grade; we went to high school following seventh grade. Eighth grade was restored by 1944.). I remember my

1

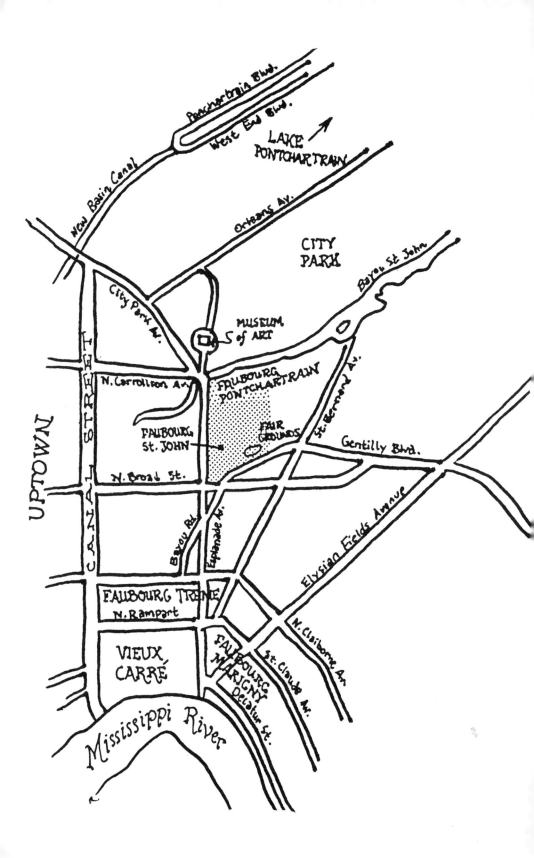

friend telling me with an air of superiority: "Uptown schools are much nicer than downtown schools, you know." On the basis of her opinion, I vainly tried to talk my family into moving uptown. My mother arched her eyebrows, pursed her lips, and shook her head as if to say, "What's got into this girl now?"

Despite these early impressions of uptown and downtown, I would like to speak up for downtown, a part of the city I now realize is richer in history, culture, and character than uptown. By downtown I mean the part of the city downriver from Canal Street to the city's boundary at St. Bernard Parish. This includes many faubourgs (suburbs), neighborhoods, and districts that have individual names and histories. The large tract of land beyond Canal Street and along the lakefront New Orleanians refer to separately from uptown and downtown. However, Lake Pontchartrain and its lakeshore played an important part in the growing-up experiences of uptowners and downtowners alike and the lake is a vital link in the history of the founding of New Orleans. (Across the river from the foot of Canal Street is Algiers, also a part of New Orleans, but so isolated when I was growing up that I didn't know of its existence until I was in college.)

Historically, New Orleans was born downtown. As early as 1708 in fact, before the founding of the city, French settlers established plantations downtown along the banks of Bayou St. John. In 1718 Jean-Baptiste Le Moyne, sieur de Bienville, the founder of New Orleans, sailed from the Gulf of Mexico into Lake Pontchartrain and up Bayou St. John to within a short distance of the Mississippi River. From the headwaters of the bayou, Bienville and his men trudged along an ancient Indian portage to the banks of the river. There Bienville chose "the beautiful crescent" of the river---a bend where the river was closest to the lake---as the site for *Nouvelle Orléans*, named for Philippe, duc d'Orléans, regent during the minority of Louix XV.

As everyone knows, that original settlement is the Vieux Carré (French for Old Quarter), commonly called the French Quarter. It is the crowning glory of downtown---of the entire city as a matter of fact; so much so that we have a separate chapter devoted to the French Quarter.

Downtown has many other districts that have contributed substantially to the city's history, culture, and architecture. The ones I know best when growing up were Faubourg Marigny and Faubourg Trémé which adjoin the French Quarter, Faubourg New Marigny, and the Faubourgs St. John and Pontchartrain which were my neighborhood.

Faubourg Marigny, on the downriver side of the Vieux Carré, was the

first of the downtown faubourgs. Many of them were called Creole faubourgs
to distinguish them from the American faubourgs on the uptown side of Canal
Street. A triangular tract of land, bounded by the river, lower Esplanade
Avenue, St. Claude Avenue and Franklin Avenue, Marigny was developed
and named after one of New Orleans' most colorful characters, Bernard Xavier
Phillipe de Marigny de Mandeville. That Creole gentleman---also a wastrel,
scoundrel and charming wit---owned just about all of downtown when his
father died in 1800; but he proceeded to lose a great part of it, squandering
his inheritance in the pursuit of pleasure. In order to raise money he subdivided a part of his plantation adjoining the city and playfully named the
streets himself, including one he called "Craps," after the game he brought
home with him following a visit to France. (Craps Street is now a continu-
ation of Burgundy Street).

The principal street of Marigny, however, is Elysian Fields, at the river
end of which stood Marigny's palatial mansion---alas, no longer there. Marigny
disregarded offers by American investors who wished to make his faubourg
a commercial center and instead sold rather small lots to his Creole friends
and relatives. His faubourg became a primarily residential area similar to the
Vieux Carré in appearance and character. Its residents included a large number
of "free persons of color" who were in the building trades. They constructed
many of the residences in the faubourg. A number of those one-story Creole
cottages and shotgun houses dating from the early 1800s still line the streets
of Marigny.

Despite its residential character, Faubourg Marigny was the site of an
exciting commercial enterprise in 1831---the building of the Pontchartrain
Railroad, one of the first in the United States. Its tracks (not removed until
the 1950s) ran along Elysian Fields from the river to the lake, a distance of
about five miles.

Soon after the railroad began operation, Bernard Marigny (probably needing
more money) decided to expand his faubourg and opened up more lots for
development behind his original subdivision along the line of the railroad tracks.
This later development was known as New Marigny.

In the latter part of the last century German immigrants flooded Faubourg
Marigny and for a while it was dubbed Little Saxony. The Germans, like all
the other immigrants who came to New Orleans, soon melded into the Creole
culture of the city.

Today one-story houses and small businesses cluster closely along the twisting, sometimes abruptly curving streets of Marigny, but when strolling through the area you occasionally come upon a delightful surprise like Washington Square. Bounded by Royal Street, Dauphine Street, Frenchmen Street and Elysian Fields, Washington Square is an inviting green oasis, reminiscent of the plazas and squares of southern European cities.

While Bernard Marigny was busy developing his faubourgs and spending his money, another important downtown faubourg, adjoining Marigny and the Vieux Carré, was coming into prominence. This was Faubourg Trémé, famous for voodoo, jazz, and Storyville. Trémé is unique for being the only settlement in the United States developed and settled primarily by free persons of color, who directed and dominated the culture, religion, economy, and architecture of the area. The community of free persons of color of New Orleans included immigrants from France and the French and Spanish colonies of the West Indies, some emancipated slaves, and children of New Orleans white men and their colored mistresses. White men maintained homes for their mistresses in Faubourgs Marigny and Trémé.

Although named for plantation owner Claude Trémé, his property makes up only one quarter of Faubourg Trémé which today runs from North Rampart Street to North Broad Street and from Canal Street to St. Bernard Avenue.

The development of Trémé began in 1810 when the city purchased Trémé's property (the faubourg was the first municipally developed suburb), but the settlement of the area reaches back to the very founding of the city when French colonists established large plantations along Bayou Road close to the ramparts of the Vieux Carré.

Over the years a colony of well-to-do French-speaking free persons of color came to dominate the faubourg. They included builders and developers, plantation owners, military officers, architects, planters, and philanthropists. Among the many notable free persons of color associated with Trémé are Henriette Delille, the quadroon founder (in 1842) of the Sisters of the Holy Family, a Roman Catholic order of nuns for black women, and Thomy Lafon, mulatto financier and philanthropist, educated in France, who left $500,000 to several charities when he died in 1893.

Far removed from the general pursuits of most free persons of color were the voodoo rites of the Negro slaves of New Orleans, performed in Faubourg Trémé's Congo Square (first called Circus Place, now called Beauregard Square). Congo Square, on North Rampart between St. Peter and St. Ann streets, was

the recreational park for the city's slaves, who gathered there on Sunday afternoons. Led by their voodoo queen, always a free woman of color, the slaves
danced to rhythmic drums and chanted songs from their native Africa. Those
sounds and rhythms formed a new kind of music that later evolved into an
original American art form---jazz.

Congo-Beauregard Square adjoins the Municipal Auditorium where I attended ballet, theater, and symphony performances when I was growing up.
The Auditorium, an Italian Renaissance structure built in 1929, is now used
mostly for high-school graduations and Carnival balls. A large residential area
next to the Auditorium was supplanted in recent years by the Louis Armstrong
Park, a recreational theme park named in honor of the famous jazz musician
who was born nearby on Jane Alley, in what is now the Central Business District.

Armstrong, "Jelly Roll" Morton and many other jazz musicians played
in Faubourg Trémé finding employment in Storyville, once the most openly
tolerated red-light district in the United States.   Storyville encompassed 38
blocks of Trémé, bounded by North Basin Street, North Robertson Street, St.
Louis Street, and Iberville Street. While Storyville's role in the evolution of jazz
has been greatly exaggerated, most jazz historians agree that the district contributed to the development of New Orleans jazz by bringing together two
important groups of musicians---the light-skinned "Creole" musicians who
lived in downtown New Orleans (primarily Trémé) and the dark-skinned "African" Negro musicians who lived in uptown New Orleans. Before these two
groups met and worked together in the sin palaces of Storyville, the downtown Negroes (descendants of the cultured free people of color) had refused
to play with the darker-skinned uptown Negroes. The collaboration of the
two groups has added to the rich heritage of New Orleans jazz.

Storyville (and jazz) was much deplored by many of the free people of
color of Trémé and there's a story that tells of Jelly Roll Morton being "kicked
out the house" when his grandmother found out he was playing in Storyville. The district flourished for twenty years from 1897 to 1917 when it
was outlawed at the request of the United States Secretary of the Navy Jo-
sephus Daniels who considered the area a threat to American seamen in New
Orleans during World War I. The Iberville Housing Project now stands on
the site of Storyville.

Much less flamboyant than Storyville are two famous landmarks of Faubourg Trémé---Our Lady of Guadalupe Church, the oldest church building

in New Orleans, and St. Louis Cemetery Number One, the oldest extant cemetery. Our Lady of Guadalupe at 411 North Rampart dates from 1826 and was New Orleans' mortuary chapel from 1827 until 1860. During those years it was against the law to hold funerals in St. Louis Cathedral in the French Quarter. New Orleanians feared contamination by the corpses of the many victims of yellow fever and cholera, two diseases that regularly decimated the city's population. Our Lady of Guadalupe Church was considered safer for funerals because at that time it lay just outside the city's ramparts. It is well known these days for ministering to the city's police and fire departments and for its promotion of devotions to St. Jude, the "saint of impossible cases."

Funeral corteges had a short march around the corner from Our Lady of Guadalupe (then known as St. Anthony's Chapel) to St. Louis Cemetery Number One for the final disposition of those yellow fever and cholera victims. Located behind the church on Basin Street at St. Louis Street, the cemetery also contains the tombs of some famous New Orleanians, including Etienne Boré, the city's first mayor, Charles Gayarré, the historian, Paul Morphy, the famous chess player, and Marie Laveau, the voodoo queen.

The white Creoles and the free colored families of Tréme both contributed to the building of St. Augustine Church at 1210 Governor Nicholls Street, the third oldest parish church in the city. It was completed in 1842 and was designed by J. N. B. De Pouilly, the architect of St. Louis Cathedral.

Cutting through Faubourg Tréme is beautiful Esplanade Avenue, a broad tree-shaded expanse which runs uninterruptedly from the river to Bayou St. John, a distance of 3.3 miles. Other historic neighborhoods along Esplanade's route include the Vieux Carré, Marigny, New Marigny, and Faubourgs St. John and Pontchartrain. Designed as a transportation link to all of these neighborhoods and a real-estate expansion to handle overflow from the Vieux Carré, Esplanade Avenue became the Creoles' answer to the Americans' development of St. Charles Avenue uptown. Early in the 1880s wealthy Creoles began building beautiful mansions along the first seven blocks of the avenue, from the river to North Rampart Street. As Esplanade was extended during the mid-nineteenth century, development continued farther out toward Bayou St. John.

Almost the entire length of Esplanade (which roughly parallels the ancient Indian portage along Bayou Road) runs through a green tunnel of oaks, elms and sycamores. Between North Broad and the bayou, the avenue has a spacious, almost rural flavor with large gardens and landscaped grounds fronting the houses and small parks every few blocks.

A number of Esplanade's mansions were designed by famous architects including Henry Howard, James Gallier, Sr., and James Gallier, Jr. A large marker at 2306 Esplanade identifies the house where French painter Edgar Degas lived when he visited relatives there during 1872-73. Degas' portrait of his sister-in-law, New Orleanian Estelle Musson, now hangs in the New Orleans Museum of Art.

Esplanade Avenue was one of our favorite strolling places when I was growing up, for it cut right through my neighborhood---the Faubourgs St. John and Pontchartrain. These two faubourgs remained an undeveloped cyress swamp until the mid-eighteen hundreds, although some sites older than the city itself lay within their boundaries. Before the French arrived to found New Orleans, a Biloxi Indian settlement and later a Houmas Indian village were situated near where I lived on Gentilly Boulevard. When the French did arrive and prepared to clear the site for the building of the city on the river bank, they established a campground for their workmen near the Houmas village at what is now Esplanade Avenue and Bayou St. John.

Bayou Road, just one block from where I lived, is the oldest passageway in New Orleans. Because it ran along a high ridge through flooded areas, it was used by the Indians and later by the earliest French explorers as a portage between Bayou St. John and the river.

By the early 1800s Faubourgs St. John and Pontchartrain were owned and subdivided by another of New Orleans' fascinating characters, Daniel Clark. An Irish immigrant and a graduate of Eton College in England, Clark became a highly successful merchant and a United States congressman. He was also suspected of collusion in the schemes of Aaron Burr and he wounded Governor William C. C. Claiborne in a duel. As colorful as Clark was, he was exceeded in eccentricity by his daughter Myra Clark Gaines, who delayed the development of Faubourgs St. John and Pontchartrain by laying claim to Clark's property---over a period of sixty years. Mrs. Gaines stayed in court all those years trying to prove herself the legitimate daughter and heir to Clark's estate. In the process, the city obtained many quitclaims from her lawyers in order to acquire clear title to the land. Eventually the city fathers succeeded in draining the swamp and developing the faubourgs.

Not far from the Faubourgs St. John and Pontchartrain, between Bayou St. John and Paris Avenue, was a neighborhood different from any other I saw as a child. Though I visited it only once I remember it clearly. It was called Pailet Lane; our maid Beulah lived there. For years I thought it was called "Pollet Land" because that's how Beulah pronounced it. Pollet Land had a scary reputation. Older kids in our neighborhood threatened younger ones by saying "the bogey man from Pollet Land is going to get you." My father once threatened to take our dog Fritzie to Pollet Land when she sneaked into the kitchen and ate a platter of perch that Beulah had fried for supper. I got a good look at Pollet Land once when my mother talked my father into going there to look for Beulah, who hadn't come to work for a week. I have never forgotten the experience. We crossed the railroad tracks at the St. Bernard Circle and were into a neighborhood that had no streets, only muddy lanes lined with little shacks made of tin and slats. Every block seemed to have a dump or a junk yard. My father stopped at several shacks asking for Beulah and was directed into still muddier lanes. When he decided that our car could go no farther he stopped at a shack with a cross on its roof and asked a big black man standing at the door if he knew Beulah. The man nodded, turned and shouted, "Hey, Beulah, someone here to see you." From a small tin shack behind the "church" Beulah emerged with a cigarette in her hand and a red bandana on her head. She came to our car, coughed a little and said "Hello, Miz Bru', Mr. Benny. Ah been sick." She looked at me in the back seat and said "How's mah l'il rosebud?" (My sister Helen was her "lily of the valley.") My mother timidly asked, "When can you come back, Beulah?" She answered, "Ah be there tomorrow." And she was. As far as I know, my father never again ventured into Pollet Land. Today Pollet Land is the site of the St. Bernard Housing Project.

St. Claude Avenue is the main artery running through the downtown section which follows the path of the river to the city's boundary with St. Bernard Parish. Much of this area, once a succession of plantations and small estates, was developed and subdivided, some of it became truck gardens and orange groves and the lower portion is now the city's main industrial corridor. One of the landmarks of this part of downtown is Jackson Barracks, which retains some vestiges of its 1835 construction. Robert E. Lee, Ulysses S. Grant, and George B. McClellan all saw duty at the barracks.

Not far beyond the city limits in St. Bernard Parish is Chalmette and the site of the Battle of New Orleans. It was a popular place for school picnics when I was in grammar school and high school. The battlefield and the beautiful line of Pakenham Oaks (named for the British general who died under them) provided an educational as well as a recreational outing.

The farther one moves downtown the stronger becomes the downtown accent, generally known as the "Yat" accent (derived from the greeting "Where y'at?"). The "Yat" accent differs from the uptown accent as much as the British accent differs from the American. The uptown area has its Irish Channel accent that strongly resembles the "Yat" accent, although local linguistic experts claim they can detect the difference easily.

When I was growing up, I had the impression that the farther one lived downtown the less desirable it was. That may have been an attitude cultivated by uptowners.

Uptown

Despite what Elsie says, uptowners were only vaguely aware of down-town's existence. Indeed, to uptown New Orleanians, downtown--with the exception of Canal Street and the Vieux Carré---might well have been another city. To the typical uptowner New Orleans *was* uptown.

This "new" section of the city lies upriver from the original French co-lonial settlement and encompasses a wide variety of neighborhoods that run the gamut from the bustle of the business district to the village atmosphere of Carrollton. Its story begins with the Faubourg St. Mary, once a part of Bienville's vast land grant, and now the site of the Central Business District just across Canal Street from the Vieux Carré. Plotted out as the city's first sub-urb in 1788, the faubourg was later settled by the Americans who flocked to New Orleans after the Louisiana Purchase. For years the newcomers were roundly snubbed by the proud, firmly entrenched Creoles who had been in the city for almost a century. The newcomers decided, therefore, to move upstream. There they carved towns and faubourgs from the plantations that lined the riverfront. In time these towns and faubourgs were incorporated into New Orleans and evolved into its uptown neighborhoods.

But first, the Americans transformed the Faubourg St. Mary into a thriv-ing community. Their friction with the Creoles continued however, finally reaching such a pitch that, in 1836, the faubourg became a separate munic-ipality. The antithesis of its Franco-Spanish neighbor, this municipality---called the American Sector---became the second of three municipalities in New Orleans; the old city was the first and Faubourg Marigny, beyond its lower boundaries, was the third. Culturally American, the new municipality was visually Anglo-Saxon, for most of its homes and buildings were designed

11

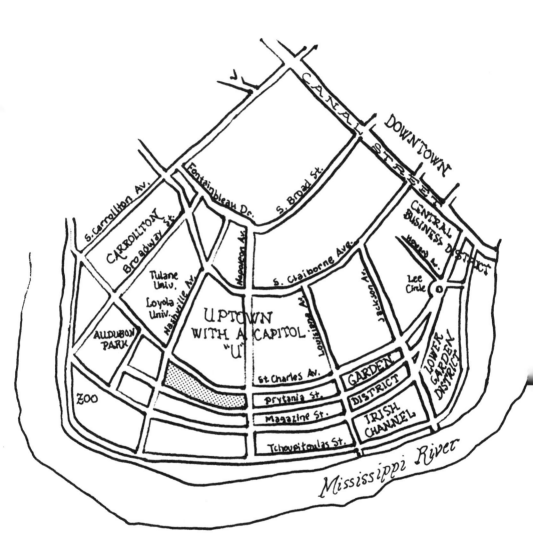

by architects who were immigrants from England, Scotland, and Ireland. At its hub, a magnificent Greek Revival city hall dominated the green expanse of Lafayette Square. Named after the Marquis de Lafayette, the French hero of the American Revolution, this square rivalled Jackson Square in the old city. Nearby, two churches soared. The First Presbyterian Church that faced the square was, at first, a Greek Revival structure, but when destroyed by fire in 1854, it was replaced by a Gothic church whose steeple---at 260 feet--- towered above the buildings in the vicinity. The other church was St. Patrick's which was established in 1833 as the first Catholic Church in New Orleans for those whose native tongue was English. Although St. Patrick's tower was visible from the Square, the church was actually a half-block away on Camp Street. In 1938, the Presbyterian Church was sold and was eventually de- molished to make way for a Federal office building. A new church, archi- tecturally reminiscent of the old one, was then built farther uptown. St. Patrick's, however, remains---its congregation dispersed by the onslaught of the business district, but its function as a church and its beauty as a building ensured by faithful friends. Today New Orleans has a new city hall, but the old city hall building, now called Gallier Hall in honor of its Irish architect, still dominates the square. A few of the municipality's side-hall brick town- houses have also survived. Some have been defaced by signs or storefronts but others, beautifully restored, emerge like pockets of history in the sky- scraper jungle that surrounds them.

Because their first settlement met with great success, the Americans con- tinued to push upstream. Their next upriver development was on the site of today's Lower Garden District. The Americans augmented the plantation homes of this rural area with plantation-type villas and houses in the Greek Revival style. But, unlike the houses of the Second Municipality, these dwell- ings were surrounded by gardens and shaded by trees. This pastoral setting was accentuated by two green, leafy squares, Coliseum and Annunciation, and punctuated by small businesses. This urban-rural setting has since be- come the typical uptown *mise en scène*. Unfortunately, many of the lovely homes of the new settlement were destined to be demolished or, escaping that, to become tenements in a slum. Lately, however, urban renewal has restored much of the lost beauty and prestige of the area, especially near Coliseum Square.

When the Livaudais plantation farther upriver was offered for sale, the way was paved for further upstream development. This plantation, when subdivided, became the core of the City of Lafayette. It was there, in the section farthest from the river, that wealthy Americans built magnificent Greek Revival mansions and enhanced them with spacious, luxuriantly land-scaped grounds. This area, now the Garden District, is, in all probability, more beautiful today than it was at its inception, for its trees and gardens have reached a ripe maturity and its mansions have attained the patina of age.

As Lafayette approached the riverfront, the residential area gradually gave way to commerce and the population became predominately Irish and German. In this section of the city, large houses surrounded by generous gardens were interspersed with small single houses, double shotgun cottages and business buildings. Many of these structures and also the sidewalks, or banquettes before them, were built from the wood of flatboats which had drifted downriver with the current and were broken up when their cargo was removed. The riverfront was lined with warehouses, wharves, and flatboat landings. Tchoupitoulas Street, the old *Chemin Royal*, that flanked it, was, in contrast to its name, a street of slaughter houses and such satellite indus-tries as soap boiling and tallow rendering. Eventually, however, the street hummed with the machinery of sawmills, foundries and cotton presses, brew-eries, ice plants, sugar refineries, and grain elevators. But as the years passed, the riverfront and its environs deteriorated into a rackety, rough and tumble area known as the Irish Channel, an area that outsiders entered at their peril. Today, however, many of its bargeboard houses have been restored and its rollicking St. Patrick's Day parade draws merrymakers from all over town.

Several miles upriver from the City of Lafayette was the City of Carrollton ---a small town which was once a popular resort. There, visitors from New Orleans arriving via steamboat or the Carrollton and New Orleans Railroad, now the St. Charles Avenue streetcar line, enjoyed the thrills of a racetrack and the amenities of the famed Carrollton Gardens Hotel. Incorporated into New Orleans in 1874, Carrollton is now the farthest upriver of the uptown neighborhoods. In many ways it has retained its rural, village charm. Its white pillared antebellum courthouse--now a school---still stands, its side streets remain quiet *cul de sacs*, its original main street, Oak Street, continues to exude the flavor of a small town shopping area and, near the riverbend, its bargeboard cottages and Victorian houses have been restored as fashionable, pastel painted shops.

Although all of the neighborhoods from the Central Business District to Carrollton are uptown, it is the section between Carrollton and the Garden District, or former City of Lafayette, that New Orleanians mean when they refer to Uptown as a proper name. This Uptown with a capital U evolved from two distinct sections. In the first section, between the Garden District and Joseph Street, plantation lands were divided into six faubourgs, including East and West Bouligny, which, in 1850, were incorporated as Jefferson City and, in 1870, became a part of New Orleans. The second section, between Joseph and Lowerline Streets, was the former Boré-Foucher plantation. First divided into small towns and subdivisions, this area, now the University Section, burgeoned after the World's Fair and Cotton Centennial Exposition which was held in 1884 and 1885 on the portion of the plantation that is now Audubon Park. Like all of uptown, Uptown with a capital U is a racially integrated mixture of socio-economic groups, of commercial neighborhoods and also of black and white residential neighborhoods that developed side by side when black domestic servants settled adjacent to the neighborhoods of their employers. Yet paradoxically, it is also a silk-stocking area which is the domain of the New Orleans upper crust. As such, Uptown is as much a state of mind as of geography. And its boundaries, thus dependent on the point of view, have no firm delineation. It is a well-known fact that New Orleanians are temperamentally insular about their city and even more so about the neighborhoods in which they live. But Uptowners are thought to be the most insular of all. Indeed, there is a saying that Uptowners consider other sections of the city foreign territory. As one, however, who was born and raised Uptown and still lives there, I regard this statement to be slightly far-fetched. But, mind you, only slightly.

My Neighborhood -
Growing Up Downtown

When I was growing up I didn't know the name of the neighborhood I lived in, it was just *my* neighborhood. Its borders were the distances my friends and I were allowed to roam until we were old enough to go further afield on the public transportation system. Within those borders our families found almost every service and sustenance needed for day-to-day living.

School, church, grocery, drugstore, shoe repair shop, dime store, movie house, barbershop, and beauty parlor all lay within walking distance of my home. Rarely did we leave our neighborhood except to go "uptown" to Canal Street for special shopping in the big department stores.

I now know, of course, that my neighborhood included the Faubourg St. John and the Faubourg Pontchartrain and that I lived just one block from the oldest street in New Orleans, Bayou Road. This was a part of downtown known as "back of town." It was in the Seventh Ward near the Fair Grounds race track on Gentilly Boulevard.

During my childhood my neighborhood was almost a microcosm of the city itself, with a rich variety of peoples and cultures. We had a small enclave of Creole families that had moved from the French Quarter and Esplanade Avenue, a few immigrant Italian families, a cross-section of middle-class New Orleanians of many national origins, and even a family that had just arrived from France. A couple of blocks from home, just around the corner from the Fair Grounds, lived several mulatto and quadroon families, some of whom were said to "pass for white" when they were in other parts of the city. One of our neighbors reported seeing one of them riding in the white section of an uptown bus. They called themselves Creoles, thus scandalizing the "real" Creoles who lived in the neighborhood. (The term Creole refers to descendants

16

of the French and Spanish colonists of New Orleans. Eventually the term expanded to describe anything owned by or associated with the Creoles--- slaves, horses, food, music, etc.)

Some of the landmarks of my neighborhood were the Fair Grounds race track, some beautiful old mansions on Esplanade Avenue, a few plantations on Bayou Road, the home of our mayor, Robert S. Maestri, on North Broad Street, and the Louisiana Jockey Club, one of the grandest buildings in New Orleans.

I lived with my parents, older brother Benny, sister Helen, and much younger brother Dan at the beginning of Gentilly Boulevard near where it intersects Bayou Road and Grand Route St. John. The mansion of that color- ful developer Daniel Clark, who once owned all of Faubourg St. John at one time stood on Bayou Road near Gentilly, very close to where I lived.

I remember Gentilly Boulevard as a wide thoroughfare lined with tall palm trees. A spacious lawn stretched from our house to the gutters edging the boulevard. The entire block across the boulevard, once the site of a street- car barn, was vacant. We flew kites and played touch football there, dodging rusted sections of streetcar tracks and other debris left behind when the barn was demolished. The city used funds from the Works Progress Administration (WPA) to convert the vacant block into a playground when I was about ten years old.

At one corner of our block was the Bell movie house and at the other, Bevinetto's grocery. A few blocks away on Esplanade avenue stood our gram- mar school, McDonogh 28. A five minute walk took us to a small commercial center on Bayou Road, the hub of which was the LeBreton Market. At one time almost all neighborhoods had the same kind of market building, which housed meat and seafood stalls, vegetable and fruit stands and poultry vendors. The buildings had cement floors covered with sawdust and they were always full of noise and bustling with activity. Most of those old markets have dis- appeared. The buildings that remain house such enterprises as weight-reducing salons or unisex barber shops. The St. Roch Market on St. Claude Avenue and the Circle Market at St. Bernard Avenue and St. Clauce Avenue are still in operation but retain little of their former liveliness. The old LeBreton market, on the site where Choctaw Indians once bartered with French set- tlers, is now dormant.

During the week we shopped at Bevinetto's grocery, but on Saturdays my mother always went to the LeBreton Market to stock up for our big week- end meals, especially for Sunday dinner. I often accompanied her. I enjoyed looking at the chickens in their cages, chasing the occasional cats that skulked about and watching the live crabs and crawfish in their big metal baskets. Once in a while a crab or a crawfish would escape and scurry across the floor, adding excitement to our shopping trip. The butcher always gave us lagniappe, usually a wiener which I peeled and ate on the walk home.

Sometimes my mother bought her chickens down the street from two poultry dealers named Guarino and Riley. Mr. Guarino and Mr. Riley both smoked cigars and wore bloody white aprons. My mother always spent a lot of time inspecting the chickens to make sure she chose a healthy one. Such indecision! Should she choose the Rhode Island Red or the Plymouth Rock? She would poke her fingers through their cage and pinch each one's breast to check their plumpness, inspect their feathers and observe their level of activity and alertness. The hapless hen that showed the greatest zest for life was soon snatched from the cage, decapitated, plucked and made ready for our Sunday table. I must have been an insensitive child because the executions of the chickens never bothered me. My sister refused to enter the poultry dealers' shop because she couldn't stand to hear the chickens flopping about in the barrel after their heads had been chopped off. My mother always insisted on inspecting the chickens even after they had been killed and cleaned. If too many innards remained, she would return the carcass for further attention. She refused to accept a chicken that had been overly bruised by its flopping about in the barrel and would pick out another. We were not popular customers. As I grew older I noticed that whenever we came to the poultry dealers, Mr. Guarino would clamp down hard on his cigar and Mr. Riley would turn and stride to the back of the store.

However, we were always welcome at Bevinetto's. Bevinetto's corner grocery store was not only the place where we bought food and other staples, it was a community center where people gathered to visit and gossip. The Bevinettos and their five children slept above the grocery, but their kitchen and living-dining room were downstairs next to the store; in fact, their family life was part of their store. A couple of chairs at the back of the store invited customers to sit and visit while Mrs. Bevinetto sliced a pound of ham or Mr. Bevinetto put up a large order of groceries for delivery. Everyone charged their groceries. The Bevinettos kept each family's charge book under the counter. Sometimes I made two or three trips in one day to Bevinetto's, depending on how well my mother had planned the day's meals. I always felt at home there, inhaling the mouth-watering aromas emanating from the kitchen and listening to the ladies swapping neighborhood gossip. Mrs. Bevinetto was always the first to know who was expecting a baby, whose husband had lost his job, or whose child had just come down with chicken pox.

The Bevinettos were a musical family. All of their children were musicians or dancers. Mr. Bevinetto played the saxophone and clarinet at the Loew's State Theater and Miss Jennie, their oldest daughter, gave me piano lessons. Another daughter, Lena, played the violin at Kolb's Restaurant. Sometimes at Bevinetto's we got not only a thin slice of ham as lagniappe but also a snatch of Paganini, Rachmaninoff, or Irving Berlin that wafted down from the upstairs practice sessions.

My favorite spot in the Bevinetto home was the dining room. It contained all kinds of family memorabilia, including pictures and stamps from Italy. The most fascinating ornament, displayed above an intricately carved oak sideboard, was a circlet of thick blond corkscrew curls (just like Shirley Temple's) held together with a pink ribbon, mounted on a layer of rosy velvet and enclosed in a gold leaf frame. Mrs. Bevinetto told me proudly that they were Miss Jennie's curls, cut when she finished high school and began giving piano lessons. Whenever I could, I slipped into the dining room for a glimpse of Miss Jennie's curls.

The Bevinettos kept a big bench outside on the corner under a china ball tree. Their neighbors would sit out there at night gossiping and sometimes listening to the radio. I remember the night they all listened to the heavyweight championship fight between Joe Louis and Max Schmeling. On that night the usually amiable group was strongly and vociferously divided. Some pulled for the German, Schmeling, calling him the great white hope. Others denounced them as traitors for not pulling for their fellow American, Joe Louis. The Louis fans also pointed out that in addition to being an American, Joe Louis had an aunt who lived in our neighborhood. I don't know whether or not this was true, but some years later Louis visited our neighborhood on a trip to New Orleans and all the boys dashed around the corner to get his autograph.

The self-proclaimed aristocrat of our block was a Creole widow who lived next door to us. She disdained almost all of our neighborhood's activities, including the gatherings at the Bevinettos. Except for her daily trips to church and to the grocery, she rarely left her house. Indeed, she rarely left her bedroom window from which she surveyed and weighed all the comings and goings of her neighbors, most of whom were usually found wanting. She was very fond of my mother and, in her way, of my whole family. She generously dispensed advice, whether solicited or not. She often pointed out to my mother the evils of public schools and was forever trying to talk her into sending me to St. Joseph's Academy on Ursulines Avenue instead of to the public John McDonogh High School. She almost stopped speaking to us when she discovered that I intended to go to Newcomb College, an institution she considered dangerous to religious faith and to personal morals. She warned my mother that girls who went to Newcomb were or became "fast". The widow delighted in talking of her ancestors. She claimed to be a descendant of Louis XIV; and she often trapped me on my way home from school and recounted to me the intricate details of her family tree. A peppery Irish lady who lived next door to us one day remarked in exasperation "What's she so proud of? Doesn't she know most of Louis XIV's children were bastards?" I believe that was the first time I'd heard that word. When I asked my mother what it meant she scolded me and told me never to say it again. Our Creole widow was most animated when she managed to collar my father on his way home from work and engage him in conversation in French. She was delighted to be speaking her "native" tongue. One day, with a sly grin, she informed me that my father did not, of course, speak Parisian French as she did. Rather, he spoke that "patois from the bayou." "He can't help it," she added generously, "that's the way he was raised." My father grew up on Bayou Lafourche near Thibodaux, in the heart of Cajun Country.

Even in non-Creole families like mine knowledge of French was considered a cultural advantage. (French culture was so strong that until 1920 there were two official languages in Louisiana and all public documents had to be published in French as well as English.) When I was in the fourth grade I began to take French lessons after school. Old Miss Reinecke came to McDonogh 28 and taught us French in the same classroom in which we had been studying reading, writing, and arithmetic all day. One day Miss Reinecke brought with her a friendly, smiling boy about 10 or 11 years old. He looked different from us. He had jet black hair and eyes, the rosiest cheeks I'd ever seen and he wore a black beret. Miss Reinecke explained that he and his family had just come from France and that they were going to make New Orleans, in fact our neighborhood, their home. He spoke no English. Miss Reinecke brought him along to make friends and to help us learn to sing the "Marseillaise."

The new family engrossed the attention of everyone in our neighborhood. We considered them exotic. We had other "foreigners" in our neighborhood, like Mr. and Mrs. Bevinetto who spoke with an accent, but their children had been born here and were a part of our neighborhood group. The little French boy, however, was soon dubbed "Frenchy" by the boys on our block, who constantly teased him about his accent, his appearance and his ignorance of things American---namely, football, marbles, rubber guns and the trading of baseball cards. I don't think he ever gained acceptance or became truly assimilated into the neighborhood. Ironically, as a college student he was as popular with girls as he had been unpopular with boys at a younger age. Friends of mine swooned over his dark good looks and his Charles Boyer accent.

Next door to Bevinetto's grocery was Joe Riggio's barbershop, another lively neighborhood meeting place. Everyone liked Joe. Besides giving haircuts and shaves, Joe listened to hard-luck stories, gave tips on the races, and told jokes all day long. There was a bookmaker across the street from the barber shop, and during the racing season Joe would run across the street to make bets. He didn't want to miss any customers, so he and the boys in our neighborhood agreed on a signal. Joe would hang a white towel on the barber shop's door when he left for the bookmaker and if a customer arrived, the boys would snatch the towel away so that Joe would hurry back to his shop.

One of Joe's favorite stories concerned a lonely young jockey who arrived in New Orleans for the 1930 racing season. He was depressed because he had "lost his bug," meaning his handicap as a novice rider. He was looking for a place to stay and Joe found him a room in our neighborhood on De Soto Street for $4.00 a week. He became Joe's friend after that and came to the barbershop for a haircut whenever he was in New Orleans. The young jockey's name was Eddie Arcaro.

As a child I never thought of the race track as a focus of sport or of gambling. To me, it was a delightful place for Sunday morning excurisons with my father. Several times during the racing season, he would waken Benny, Helen, and me early on a Sunday morning, stuff our pockets with sugar cubes and walk us down to the Fair Grounds, just two blocks from our house. My brother Dan, almost eleven years my junior, does not figure in my early childhood reminiscences. As we walked through the open gate I always felt a rush of excitement. The racetrack was quiet except for the faint thud of horses' hooves, a sound that grew louder as we approached the track. By the time we were close enough for my father to lean on the railing, the hooves sounded like thunder. Two or three horses, on their early morning exercise, would gallop by, throwing up mud or dust in their wake, the grunts and cries of their jockey trailing behind. We would walk along the track watching other horses exercise until our excitement abated.

Then we would come to my favorite part of the racetrack excursion. We would stroll past the stalls, admiring the horses and chatting with the stable hands. When we got a particularly friendly reception, my father would ask if we could feed the horse some sugar cubes. I was always slightly apprehensive but thrilled when I put out my palm and felt the warm, soft, tickling nibble of the horse's lips as the sugar lump disappeared. I considered the feeding of sugar cubes the height of equine enjoyment until the morning a particularly affable stable hand asked if we would like to sit on his horse. We were beside ourselves and squealed so much that I think the poor man must have regretted his rash offer. He hoisted us up, however, first me and then Helen (Benny wasn't with us that day) and led the horse slowly up and down in front of the stable. It was the most memorable and exciting horseback ride I ever had.

There were other animals at the race track, too. Almost every stable hand had a pet dog, bird, or monkey. We looked forward to visiting certain stalls, to see not only the horses but also their pet companions. A feisty parrot who softly sqawked "And they're off" over and over was my favorite.

Our visit to the Fair Grounds wasn't complete until we walked across the track to the beautiful green infield where we paid our respects at the grave of the famous racehorse Black Gold. This courageous colt rivalled "Black Beauty" as a childhood favorite after my father told us of Black Gold's short but glorious career. A Cinderella horse, spawned from a royal Kentucky stallion and a plebeian mare owned by an Oklahoma Indian, Black Gold won four derbies, including the Kentucky Derby (in 1924). He ran his first race at the Fair Grounds and tragically, his last, when he broke a leg and had to be destroyed. My father was in the stands the day the tragedy happened on January 8, 1928. When he told us the story the first time he had a catch in his throat and we all had tears in our eyes.

My neighborhood was a stronghold of the Old Regular political organization. Although I was not much aware of politics as a child, I vividly remember the assassination of Huey Long. We heard the "Kingfish's" song "Every Man a King" on the radio all the time and I sometimes heard Huey himself holding forth in loud, strident tones. He had lots of ideas about how to end the Depression and his promise of "a chicken in every pot" made him the friend of the poor and the jobless.

I was vaguely aware that my mother did not like Huey Long and disapproved of my father attending occasional Old Regular crab and shrimp boil parties. The Old Regulars were supporters of Huey Long.

I woke up the morning of September 9, 1935 to blaring radio announcements and loud, agitated voices in the street. I knew immediately something terrible had happened. Everyone looked so worried and some of the women were wringing their hands and crying. Long had been shot the night before in the state capitol and as the news worsened during the day concerning his chances of survival, some people jumped in their cars and drove to Baton Rouge to keep vigil at the hospital there. Long died early on the morning of September 10. A wave of shock and disbelief swept the neighborhood. While Long was considered a dictator and tyrant by many New Orleanians—especially those in the uptown "silk stocking" district—he was a hero to most of the people in my neighborhood. They mourned Huey Long as they mourned for members of their own family.

The Louisiana scandals following the assassination of Long were so much a part of radio and newspaper coverage that even I—young and unaware as I was—could not help but be aware of them. What most shocked me at the time was the revelation of the wrongdoing of the president of Louisiana State University, Dr. James Monroe Smith. I'll never forget his name. I avidly followed the story of his disappearance and flight to Canada and eventual arrest—documented with a front-page picture of him in the *Times-Picayune* in the custody of federal agents. For some reason the involvement of a university president in such nefarious goings-on seemed more scandalous to me than any of the other revelations.

Almost everyone in our neighborhood had a "colored girl" who worked as a maid two or three times a week. Our family was one of the few that had a full-time household servant. Our "girl" Beulah came to our house six days a week, arriving in time to make breakfast and staying until after supper. When we were little she walked us to and from school and took us on errands with her to the grocery store or to the market.

One Mardi Gras when my mother was sick and Dad had to work, Beulah took Helen and me to the Rex parade on Canal Street. Instead of walking to Canal Street with lots of our neighbors as we usually did, we took the Broad Street bus. We sat in the back with Beulah behind the movable marker that separated white and colored passengers. (We called the marker a "screen.") Although I had noticed the buses' seating arrangements before, they had never dented my consciousness as this particular experience did. At first Helen and I felt strange, but the colored people sitting with us were friendly and admired our costumes and soon we were all talking together. We felt right at home.

Later when I was older and traveling on the bus alone I always felt embarrassed if I had to move the "screen" when I sat down.

We had a free and easy relationship with Beulah. She often intervened when my mother threatened to spank or punish us. She made excuses for us and enumerated our virtues (she had a great imagination). She was such a part of our household that when she left us during World War II to take a better paying job in a laundry, our house seemed quiet and incomplete without her huge frame bustling in the kitchen or singing at the ironing board.

My friendship with Beulah was marred only once when I was about 12 years old. I had been to see "Gone with the Wind" and I was much impressed with Mammy addressing Scarlett as "*Miss* Scarlett." One day I ventured to say to Beulah that I was now old enough for her to start calling me "*Miss* Elsie." She was at the ironing board, pressing the white pleated skirt I wore to church. She glared at me, handed me the iron and said "If you old enough for that, you old enough to iron yo' own skirt." I quickly assured her that I was only joking and that was the end of that.

In her spare time Beulah listened to the soap operas on the radio and carefully chose her lottery numbers. Although lotteries had been outlawed in New Orleans since 1898, they hadn't disappeared. In fact they seemed to be, like bookmaking, all but legal when I was a child. Lottery companies flourished and Beulah was an avid player of the numbers. She often brought a dream book to our house and asked me to read it to her so she could choose her numbers according to her dreams. Beulah knew all kinds of "gigs" or lottery formulas of three numbers. I learned about "angel gigs," "blood gigs," "brother-in-law gigs," "Chinaman gigs," and many other exotic-sounding formulas. Sometimes Beulah played the "Washerwoman's gig," the numbers 4, 11, and 44 a formula which once won a fortune for its lucky player. My mother disapproved of the lottery and my part in Beulah's participation in it, so Beulah and I usually talked lottery when Mother was absent. Once in a while I slipped a nickel to Beulah to buy a lottery ticket for me, but I never picked a lucky gig. Mother often pointed out to Beulah that she couldn't really win at playing the numbers and that the lottery companies were all crooked, but Beulah was always convinced that her next bet would buy her a ticket to Chicago. Chicago was her idea of heaven. Why, I don't know. She had never been out of New Orleans. Besides my mother's prejudice against gambling on moral grounds, she also frowned on Beulah's participation for practical reasons. When Beulah occasionally failed to show up for work, Mother complained that Beulah had probably collected on her lottery ticket and decided to celebrate her good luck.

I now realize that gambling must have been pervasive in our neighborhood, as it was throughout New Orleans. Our neighborhood's gambling activities included bookmaking, lottery, church bingo, and even a weekly floating poker game. The poker game came to light once when news flew through the neighborhood that the police had raided Bevinetto's grocery store. Mr. and Mrs. Bevinetto were not their usual cheery selves that week and I noticed that for several weeks afterward the box of poker chips I usually saw on the sideboard beneath Miss Jennie's curls was missing. One day it reappeared and I suppose that the poker game then resumed.

We had a lot of exotic pets when we were growing up. My brother Benny's favorite was his alligator, Alley Oop. We often bought little alligators and turtles at the dime store on Bayou Road, as did a lot of other kids at that time. The alligators and turtles usually died or disappeared within a couple of weeks. Alley Oop got much attention and care, however, and thrived, growing from a skinny six-inch baby to a rugged two-and-a-half foot adolescent. He lived in a pen in our back yard, occasionally digging his way out and terrorizing our Airedale, Fritzie. Once Alley Oop grabbed Fritzie by the tail. She ran around the yard yelping, with the alligator swinging behind and holding on for dear life until Benny freed Fritzie's tail. Benny made a leash for Alley and often took him walking up and down the banquette and around the block. The neighbors soon got over their initial interest in that spectacle but motorists on Gentilly Boulevard would sometimes slow down or stop to get a better look. Whenever it rained enough for the gutters to fill, we would all wade in them and Benny would treat Alley to a swim. One day when the water was especially high and Alley was feeling especially frisky, he broke his leash and disappeared. Benny searched frantically while the rest of us scrambled for safer ground. Alley was gone for good, probably finding his way into the sewer system and thence into one of New Orleans' many canals. Years later we read about an eight-foot alligator that had been found in one of the drainage canals and we wondered if it was Alley.

In addition to Alley, we had flying squirrels, guinea pigs, turtles, ducks, and an alligator gar. We kept the gar in a pond in our back yard. Our favorite pet for 13 years, however, was our faithful dog Fritzie. Fritzie roamed our neighborhood, making friends in each block. When Fritzie was hit by a car and we nursed her back to health, her admirers visited her every day; one of them was an old man who called her Nellie and considered her to be his pet. It turned out that Fritzie used to visit him every afternoon for delectable treats like liver and soup bones. Fritizie was a streetwise dog. Her nemesis was the dog-catcher. The dog wagon passed through our neighborhood once every two or three weeks on a Saturday morning, picking up strays and any other four-footed creatures on the loose. When someone spotted the wagon, the signal went from house to house. Kids poured forth to round up their pets before the dog-catcher did.

The dog-catcher had a grudge against Fritzie because she had caused him to lose a whole wagonload of dogs one Saturday morning. On that particular morning, the dog-catcher had corralled a little terrier that belonged to one of our neighbors. He was opening the wagon's gate to thrust the terrier inside when Fritzie dashed from under our house and grabbed his ankle. Not only did he let go of the terrier but he failed to close the door of the wagon as he reached down to protect himself. He was immediately engulfed and bowled over by an avalanche of dogs dashing madly for freedom. In the melee, Fritzie made her getaway but became the major target of every dog-catching expedition thereafter. We had to bail her out of the pound several times during her adventurous life.

When I was about 12 years old, I decided to train Fritzie after seeing a "Lassie" movie. When I came home from school I put her through the paces of "heeling" and "staying" in the backyard. Then I got a leash and walked her around the block. Those drills amused some of our neighbors who were accustomed to seeing Fritzie roam at will. Fritzie indulged my whim, however, and tolerated our daily walks, perhaps aware that the walks were a passing fancy.

My friends and I often took walks around our neighborhood. When we were little and first allowed to roam beyond our own block we called our walks "exploring." Our favorite destination was Esplanade Avenue because of its huge live oaks and mansions. The novelty of roaming freely (within our neighborhood's bounds, of course; we were not allowed to cross Esplanade Avenue) entertained us during several "explorations." Then we began to look for adventure, something different or unexpected. One day we turned at a little street called Leda and found it. There in the middle of the block stood an elaborately ornamented mansion unlike anything we had ever seen before. We stopped in our tracks and gawked. We felt as though we had wandered into a fairy tale. This mansion seemed as tall as the Maison Blanche department store on Canal Street, dwarfing the mansions on Esplanade Avenue. It rose four stories high, decorated with terraces and archways, a grand staircase, ornate windows and a large, fanciful cupola on its roof. The lush gardens surrounding it seemed untended.

We came home still excited with our new discovery. My mother didn't know much about the marvelous mansion but that night my father told us its story. The mansion had served for many years as a clubhouse for the Louisiana Jockey Club. The Club had developed the Fair Grounds race track which was next door to the mansion. My father said the Jockey Club's members used to watch the races from its balconies and rooftop. In it, they entertained prominent visitors to the city, including Grand Duke Alexis Romanoff of Russia on his famous visit to New Orleans during the Carnival season of 1872. (It was the Grand Duke who inspired the adoption of Mardi Gras' theme song "If Ever I Cease to Love"--"May oysters have legs and cows lay eggs if ever I cease to love." The song and Lydia Thompson, the pretty actress who sang it, were both favorites of the playboy Grand Duke.)

I later discovered that the Jockey Club had originally been the Luling Mansion, built by famous New Orleans architect James Gallier, Jr., for wealthy businessman Florence Luling in 1865 and was patterned after a French chateau. The building and grounds covered ten acres. The mansion still stands, with only a touch of its former grandeur, hemmed in by smaller structures and sadly neglected.

Almost as enchanting as the Luling Mansion, though not so exotic to us, was a lovely two-story house at 2257 Bayou Road. When I attended John McDonogh High School on Esplanade Avenue I often passed by the Benachi-Torre House (as a plaque in front of the house now designates it) on my way home. I'd look through its beautiful ironwork fence at the fountain in the yard and imagine that the house was once a big plantation. The Creole cottage that stood next door to it I decided must have been the overseer's house. So much for daydreaming. The real story is that this Greek Revival mansion was built in 1859 for Nicholas Benachi, wealthy merchant and Greek consul in New Orleans. It was later owned by the Torre family who lived in it when I used to pass by and admire it. It was never a plantation. The next door cottage is known as the Fleitas House and was built in the early 1800s. Both buildings have beautiful, spacious grounds and are now considered outstanding landmarks in the city.

We didn't have to go exploring to find interesting sights and sounds. A variety of them passed in front of our house almost every day. We knew the usual peddlers, such as the scissors and knife sharpeners, the umbrella man, the fruit and vegetable hawkers and the egg lady. My favorites were the clothes pole man and "Poke Chop Mary." Poke Chop Mary passed by every Saturday morning selling pralines and little fruit pies. She was a grumpy little colored woman always dressed in an ankle-length gingham dress and a poke bonnet. She had no vendor's cry and she needed none. Her pralines and pies were so good that as soon as she hobbled into view children ran inside to beg a nickel or dime to buy some of her goodies. She dispensed them grudgingly and never responded to our enthusiastic greetings, as other vendors did. I liked the clothes pole man because he looked just like his wares---tall, skinny and knobby. He wore a derby hat and shouted at the top of his lungs, "Clothes poles, I got the clothes poles, lady, sellin' clothes poles a nickel and a dime."

The egg lady was a tiresome chatterbox. A big, redheaded woman with a coarse voice and flushed cheeks, she insisted on expounding the virtues of her yard eggs to us even though my mother was one of her regular customers and needed no endorsements. The egg lady would hold aloft a large brown egg between her thumb and forefinger and exclaim, "*This* is a *real* egg. Those things you buy in the grocery store aren't real eggs. But this, *this* is a real egg!"

Once or twice a year photographers appeared in our neighborhood with a pony or a goat cart, enticing children to have their picture taken. Almost every downtown family in New Orleans must have a photograph album containing snapshots of boys and girls smiling from atop a tired pony or at the reins of a gaily painted goat cart.

When I was growing up each neighborhood in New Orleans had (as it still has) a unique character. At that time each was a self-contained, independent community, and when you left your own neighborhood you knew you were in a different milieu. Shortly after I finished college, my family moved uptown. I didn't think about my childhood neighborhood for many years. The perspective of those intervening years has revealed to me what a culturally rich and colorful little community it was. It was a good place to grow up, at least for all of us who felt like we belonged there. I don't know about "Frenchy," the little boy from France who never quite fit in. He grew up to be a successful phychiatrist.

Uptown with a Capital "U"

When I was a child I lived with my mother, my father and brother, my maternal grandfather and three uncles in the section of uptown New Orleans referred to by the proper name Uptown. Our street, Prytania, was, like other streets in the neighborhood, flanked by towering live oaks, vintage Victorian houses, and gardens brimming with crepe-myrtle trees, azaleas, camellias, rose bushes, and beds of old-fashioned flowers. In those days there was a rural quality about Uptown which made growing up there tantamount to growing up in a small country town. Roosters crowed at dawn, four-o'clocks grew wild, iron picket fences were a froth of honeysuckle vines and many streets, still unpaved, were lined by ditches where black-eyed Susans grew and by brick sidewalks broken by the thrust of ancient tree roots.

To me, this sylvan setting was a universe in miniature, a Lilliputian world potent with the thrill of discovery, yet so familiar it was almost a part of my bones. It was by walking that I grew to know and love it. Mother and Daddy took great pleasure in walking and introduced me to it at an early age. Even as a toddler I found a walk to be a great adventure. My early walks proceeded through a world that teemed with doodle bugs and lady bugs, lizards, mosquito hawks, fairy rings, and tiny, hidden flowers. In this magic land of childhood, I could indulge my fantasies and be a daisy or a butterfly, an elephant or an ant. But as I grew tall, telescoping away from the ground on which I walked, I became increasingly aware of the everyday world of our neighborhood.

Across from the Prytania Streetcar Barn, just two blocks from our house, there was a small community of stores. The ones we patronized most often were the market, the delicatessen, the bakery and the drugstore. The drugstore was my favorite and, for that matter, the favorite of all the children

29

in the neighborhood. The milkman and the vegetable man stopped by our house each day and Mother ordered groceries on the telephone, but it was up to Rosie, our cook, to go to market to buy seafood, fish, or meat. Every morning she tied on a clean apron, slipped a basket over her arm, and walked to the Prytania Market. Sometimes she invited me to tag along. This was always a treat, for the sights, the sounds, and even the smells of the market fascinated me. Caged chickens squawked, crabs scurried in big vats, pyramids of oysters exuded the salt tang of the sea and wooden stalls overflowed with fruits and vegetables. Customers haggled, scales jingled, cash registers clanged, and occasionally a stray cat sneaked through the door and darted underfoot. Even the floor had a touch of the exotic for, like the circus floor, it was covered with sawdust.

Upon leaving the market, we stopped at the bakery, a quiet store whose glass cases were filled with rolls, buns, loaves of bread and many tempting confections. Although Rosie was a prolific baker of cakes and pies, cookies and biscuits, she drew the line at baking bread. She sometimes made corn-bread, but that was as far as she would go. The French bread that was a staple of our meals came directly from the bakery. Sandwich bread was anathema to Rosie. She not only refused to buy it, she refused to have it in the house. But on Sundays when she took the evening off, Mother and Daddy, like naughty children, always bought a loaf of the offending bread along with other supper supplies at the delicatessen. It was a rare Monday morning when any of the bread was left over, but, when it was, Rosie registered her disapproval by feeding it to the chickens we kept in the backyard.

As I grew older, I became a great fan of the movies. There was a picture show, the Prytania, just up the street from our house. On Friday nights when the serial was playing and the feature film was rated A for children, Brother and I were usually a part of the high-spirited juvenile audience. The walk to and from the movies was almost as exciting as the show itself. In the dark, familiar landmarks cast mysterious shadows and Brother and his cohorts took advantage of the situation by hiding behind bushes, then jumping out and screaming "Boo!"

Although I loved the movies, I loved movie stars even more. It was a great thing for me, therefore, that a real, live movie star lived around the corner. Her name was Marguerite Clark. I had never seen her in the movies because she was a star of the silent screen who, according to Mother, gave up her career when she married Harry P. Williams, a pioneer aviator and the scion of a wealthy lumber family, and moved to New Orleans. She lived on St. Charles Avenue in a palatial, neo-Italianate mansion, now the Milton S. Latter Memorial Library, which occupies a whole block of beautifully landscaped grounds. I walked past her house almost every day and, for years, I scrutinized it, hoping for a glimpse of one of the dazzling Hollywood luminaries I saw at the Prytania. But alas, I hoped in vain.

Dorothy Dix, famous for her advice to the lovelorn, was another Uptown celebrity. She lived in an elegant house on Prytania Street which, though palladian, was small compared to Miss Clark's. We invariably passed it upon entering Audubon Park, for we used the Prytania Street entrance to the park rather than the imposing main entrance on St. Charles Avenue. We always drove to the park in order to save our energy and our legs for long walks when we arrived. Many of our walks were necessary treks between the flying horses (the carousel), the zoo, the aquarium, the sea lion pool, the swanboat and the miniature train. We often walked, however, with no thought of a destination, but simply for the joy of walking. One of our favorite walks was beside the bridle path. To a small child, this walk was like a journey through a deep, mysterious wood. Huge live oaks trailing mossy banners formed an arch above our heads and, at our feet, their gnarled roots stretched and coiled like tentacles. In this magic wood, strawberries, violets, and ferns grew wild, squirrels scampered, and crawfish occasionally peeped above their mudholes. As we walked, Daddy told us fascinating tales about the wonders of the natural world. It wasn't until much later that I recognized these stories for the scientific lectures---geared, of course, to youthful minds---that they really were.

Another favorite walk was along the shore of the lagoon. This walk was as delightful as a stroll through open countryside. Across the water, beyond a fringe of trees and shrubs, the golf course fanned out like a meadow. The lagoon, itself, was picturesque and also a scene of great activity. A flatboat called *The Swanboat* by virtue of the wooden swans upon its prow, chugged back and forth, its passengers waving to fishermen, picnickers and pedestrians along the shore. Keeping it company were skiffs and canoes, flotillas of swans and whole families of ducks. Brother and I loved to feed the ducks and were always well supplied with stale bread for their delectation. As we walked towards St. Charles Avenue we could see the square Gothic tower of Most Holy Name of Jesus Church soaring above the treetops. This lovely view reminded me of a picture in one of my storybooks. It was a picture of an English scene, and to this day, the view of Holy Name's tower as seen from the lagoon puts me in mind of England.

Yet nothing could have been more typical of the South than Audubon Park. It was, in fact, the core of the vast Foucher-Boré plantation.   Jean Etienne Boré was a French aristocrat who settled in New Orleans in the eighteenth century and Foucher was his son-in-law. Boré was the city's first mayor after the Louisiana Purchase. He also perfected the process of granulating sugar commercially in Louisiana. All of this we learned from Mother. For although Daddy took us to the park, treated us to its "rides" and told us about its flora and fauna, it was Mother who told us about its history. We learned from her that some of Andrew Jackson's troops were billeted on the plantation lands before the Battle of New Orleans and that during the Civil War first a Confederate and then a Union encampment was located there and after the war, a Union hospital. We also learned that the World's Fair and Cotton Centennial Exposition took up a large portion of the site in 1884 and '85. The fair's main building covered thirty acres and its Horticulture Hall was alleged to be the largest glass conservatory in the world. Yet, by the time we frequented the park only two remnants of the fair remained, and one was just a name: the row of imposing houses that overlooked the bridle path was called Exposition Boulevard. The other remnant was the huge brown "meteorite" on the golf course which was plainly visible from the arched bridge that spanned the lagoon. In later years I learned, to my dismay, that the "meteorite" was really a boulder of iron ore left over from the geological exhibit of the fair. Daddy, I realized, must have known this all along but, despite his respect for scientific truth, didn't have the heart to disillusion us. For Brother and I were wild about the "meteorite." Indeed, we stood in awe of it. After all, it was our only link with outer space.

I loved to walk on St. Charles Avenue. The Avenue, as we called it, was Uptown's most prestigious street as well as its main thoroughfare. Intersected by a grassy, tree-lined neutral ground and flanked by stately homes and spacious lawns, the Avenue was as lovely as a garden. From time to time, however, its serenity was invaded by the passing of a St. Charles Avenue streetcar. These streetcars, now placed on the National Register of Historic Places by virtue of their descent from an early nineteenth-century railroad, rattled up and down the neutral ground on their way "around the belt"---that is, from Canal Street to Canal Street in a wide circle that included St. Charles Avenue, Carrollton Avenue and Tulane Avenue.

Uptown's side streets were, for the most part, enclaves of Victorian frame houses, but the Avenue was a panorama of far-ranging architectural materials and styles. Victorian mansions embellished with turrets, porches, *porte co-chères,* stained-glass windows and beveled-glass front doors vied for pride of place with mansions of the neo-Italianate, Greek Revival, Georgian, Romanesque, and Louisiana cottage styles.

Although I passed many beautiful homes on the Avenue when going back and forth to school, my favorites were two great mansions which, like Marguerite Clark's, piqued my imagination. One was the Orleans Club, an exclusive women's club housed in a French-Empire-style house enhanced by ironwork reminiscent of the Vieux Carré. Occasionally a white canvas awning was unfurled before the club. Stretching like a snowcapped tunnel across the lawn, over the sidewalk and onto the curb, it was the herald of exciting events such as wedding receptions and debutante dances and teas. I invariably felt a thrill when I walked through its sidewalk openings and, peering through its dusky depths, imagined myself as a debutante or a bride. Mother often went to parties at the club and, knowing she had an interested audience, told me about them afterwards. Like a child whose face is pressed to the window of a candy store, I drank in every word, longing for the day when I would experience such festivities first hand.

Around the corner from the Orleans Club was the elegant Soniat-Dufossat plantation house where Miss Lilian Lewis conducted classes in ballroom dancing. I attended her classes reluctantly. To begin with I didn't care to dance and, to go on with, I considered it an imposition to be required to do so with a boy. At the beginning of each class, the boys, completely out of character in coats and ties, lined up on one side of the room and the girls, starched and beribboned, lined the other. A great deal of hostility was generated between these two camps, for most of us were there against our will. Miss Lewis, however, seemed oblivious to our sulks and scowls and, against all odds, eventually taught us to dance.

My other favorite Avenue house was a massive mansion built of rough-hewn stone. The romantic medieval style of its facade never failed to spark expectations of more captivating sights inside. Although one of my classmates lived in this delightful house and often invited me there to play, its interior remained a mystery, for we always played outside.

When our Avenue walks were in the opposite direction from school, it meant that we were going to visit Daddy's mother in Richmond Place. These walks took us farther uptown in the direction of Audubon Park and, just across from it, Tulane and Loyola Universities and Holy Name of Jesus Church.

Upon reaching the Avenue, I always insisted on immediately crossing over to its far side. For there, beside the *porte cochère* of a large white Victorian house (since demolished), was a brightly painted statue of Red Riding Hood and, facing her ferociously, a statue of the wolf. This potentially dangerous situation, forever frozen in the center of a flowerbed, was to Brother and me and, indeed, to all the children in the neighborhood, the most enchanting sight on the Avenue.

Across the neutral ground there was a Spanish mission-style house that always caught my eye and along with it my fancy. Next came two tremendous brick buildings, each set back beyond sweeping lawns and occupying a city block. Gilbert Academy, a black preparatory school, was situated where New Orleans University, the first black university in the city, once stood. Beyond it was the Jewish Children's Home. Although the home was renowned for its excellence, its exterior was rather forbidding. As a result, whenever I passed it I felt a surge of gratitude that I had a home and family of my own. The modern buildings of De La Salle High School---a Catholic school for boys---and the Jewish Community Center have now replaced those of the Academy and the Home.

A block farther uptown, at the corner of Octavia Street, there was a tree-shaded greensward called Danneel Park. Daddy always stopped there awhile so that Brother and I could run around and, as he put it, blow off steam. At this point we were only three blocks from the street where we would take a right turn off the Avenue towards Richmond Place. It was there, at the entrance to Rosa Park, that my dream house stood. This magnificent white-frame mansion was the quintessential turn-of-the-century Avenue home. Embellished with white marble stairs and gallery, a doorway glittering with leaded, beveled glass and wooden flower garlands festooning the frieze and the columns of its porch and *porte cochère*, it was as lovely as a Valentine. When Daddy finally decided that I had stared long enough at its elegant facade, we turned off the Avenue into Rosa Park. This tranquil street with its imposing homes and broad, landscaped neutral ground led into Everett Place which in turn led to Richmond Place where my grandmother lived. All three of these private, parklike streets seemed miles away from the clanging streetcars and automobile traffic of St. Charles Avenue. Indeed, they sometimes seemed miles away from Uptown. For although Uptown had a rural flavor, it also had the bustle of a small country town.

The Convent

My school was one of the most beautiful landmarks Uptown or, for that matter, along St. Charles Avenue. Officially The Academy of the Sacred Heart, it was also known as the Rosary. But those who knew and loved it often bypassed both names, affectionately calling it "The Convent."

The convent was a mellow turn-of-the-century brick building that not only housed the school but also a soaring Gothic chapel and the cloister of the nuns. Surrounded by broad, white-columned galleries, it was, and still is, set like a jewel amidst a grassy, tree-shaded garden with a fountain playing at the center of a circular drive. This lovely facade was echoed inside by spacious, high-ceilinged rooms, gleaming hardwood floors and tall, gracefully arched windows through which the daylight poured.

Like all convents of the Sacred Heart, the convent was a school *par excellence*. Yet it was much more than a school. It was a home away from home. The family feeling it generated was so strong that the nuns were our mothers and we were their children. We even called them Mother. I remember the feeling of reassurance that familiar name evoked in us, especially in apprehensive little fledglings new to school.

Our relationship with the nuns was one of mutual affection and respect. The curtsy was a traditional sign of our respect. It was one of the first skills we learned at school. Dropping a curtsy was a brand new experience for the four-year-olds of the primer, and its mastery was a source of much hilarity. At first we tumbled and toppled about like so many roly-polys, but before long we could curtsy smoothly and with budding grace. Through the years we dropped hundreds of curtsies. Some were stylized salutations reserved

35

for grand occasions, but most were quick salutes to superior authority when-ever encountered in the person of a nun.

Life at Sacred Heart had a decided Gallic flavor. The Society of the Sacred Heart, founded by St. Madeleine Sophie Barat in Grenoble, France, in 1800, was rooted in the soil of France, a circumstance which made its convents French in spirit if not, indeed, in fact. We were introduced to French along with the curtsy and struck up a rapport with it that lasted from the primer through high school and sometimes even beyond our convent days. French words crept naturally into our conversations. The snack served to the boarders each day at three o'clock was *goûter,* the holidays we celebrated at school were *congés,* and the game of hide-and-seek that was their highlight was *cache-cache. Primes* was a Monday assembly at which our weekly conduct was assessed. Our fate was sealed on small cards called *notes,* ceremoniously dispensed to us by Reverend Mother. These cards were labelled---in descending order---*très bien* (very good), *bien* (good), and *assez bien* (acceptable). The sinner who received no card had *pas de notes,* or, as we put it, "lost her notes," which meant that she was guilty of some heinous crime like smoking on the school grounds or, God forbid, leaving the grounds without permission.

Aside from French we had a language of our own at Sacred Heart. "Halls" were "corridors," the "cafeteria" was a "refectory" and the "auditorium," an "assembly room." The "bookstore" was a "bazaar," "recess" was "recre-ation," and "classes," divided into three groups of four, were "Primaries," "Preparatories" and "Academics." Our "teachers" were "class mistresses." We were surveilled by a "mistress of study hall," and our aches and pains were tended by an "infirmarian" (nurse). Lay nuns, called Sisters, cleaned and polished the convent to perfection and cooked for the religious community and the boarders. To this day I can recall the tantalizing aroma of the boarders' hot lunch. One whiff was enough to bring tears to the eyes of sandwich-toting day students.

A uniform was an integral part of our convent days. Indeed we were often reminded that when in uniform we were representatives of Sacred Heart and should conduct ourselves accordingly. Turned-down socks, hiked-up skirts and pulled-out blouses were out of the question during school hours. We were also on our honor to forego such dishabille once outside the con-vent gates. However, on this point our sense of honor was rarely as it should have been.

On formal occasions we wore white uniforms which, in contrast to our everyday attire, made us feel quite gorgeous. Short white cotton gloves were *de rigueur* with white uniforms. Since they were also *de rigueur* for *Primes*, white glove inspection was a frequent Monday event. Anticipating this, we often took our gloves home for a weekend wash. There were, however, a few free spirits who occasionally turned their less-than-white gloves inside out and skipped the laundry detail.

Ribbons, wide sashes worn across the shoulder and fastened at the waist, were a part of the uniform that few were privileged to wear. They were honors given to the girls most outstanding in dependability and leadership. These girls not only wore ribbons but were also called Ribbons. Pink Ribbons were small girls in the Primaries, Green Ribbons were in-between girls in the Preparatories and Blue Ribbons, the most prestigious of all, were young ladies(?) in the Academics.

A minimum of jewelry was tolerated at the convent but makeup was forbidden. Yet by the time we reached the Academics it was obvious the nuns believed we became painted women on the weekend.

Makeup inspection was the rule on Monday morning as we left the Academic Study Hall for our first class of the day. The mistress of study hall, at other times a great favorite, stood behind a small table by the door and scrutinized our hands and faces as we passed warily before her. On the table was a bottle of nail-polish remover, a jar of cold cream and a box of facial tissues. If our fingernails or faces glowed with the slightest trace of artificial color, the offending hue was promptly and efficiently removed. Make-up, we were reminded, was *not* a part of the uniform.

Festive occasions that were white-uniform, white-glove affairs punctuated the school year. Although often celebrations of religious feasts, they also marked such school events as the year-end Distribution of Prizes and sometimes even honored the nuns themselves. Both Reverend Mother and the Mistress General (headmistress) had feast days of their own which, to our delight, were always followed by a *congé*.

The highlight of a feast day was a formal assembly called Feast Wishes. It took place in the assembly room, flower filled for the occasion, with the whole school in attendance. Tableaux (living pictures), songs, addresses, and bouquets were essential ingredients of this event. So was the curtsy. However, the quick up-and-down curtsy that we dropped each day was metamorphosized into an elegant obeisance for the Feast Wishes. As Reverend Mother entered the room we all curtsied deeply and together, as precision perfect as Rockettes. This curtsy was a notable achievement, for we ranged in height from tall to tiny, and long legs had to match the range of short ones. However, we were soon treated to a solo curtsy that cast our group curtsy into the shade.

At the height of the Feast Wishes one of the Academics, usually a Blue Ribbon, walked to the center of the room carrying a sheet of paper from which a bright cascade of ribbons fell. This was an address she was to read, the keynote, so to speak, of the occasion. When she was directly opposite Reverend Mother, she swept a court curtsy that took her right down to the highly polished floor. This performance was a ballet feat, the epitome of dexterity and grace. Yet to us, the fascinated audience, it was a thriller. We held our breaths, in fact, until she was once more perpendicular.

There were many feasts in honor of the Blessed Virgin, but in May, her special month, the beauty of the season seemed to merge with our devotion to her. Each morning we came to school with arms full of flowers fresh picked from our gardens. These fragrant, bright bouquets were heaped upon Our Lady's altar and before her statues in the study halls and corridors. This display of floral fervor increased each day until it climaxed in the May Crowning on the last day of the month. The Crowning was a flowery procession whose high point was the placing of a wreath of spring flowers on Mary's statue as a token and a symbol of our love. Yet, despite our fondness for giving her flowers, our most outstanding gift was the keeping of the May Practice. This was a gift that cost us dearly, for we were chatter-boxes, and the May Practice was Silence. Silence was required of us at certain times and places, but the actual keeping of silence was often a losing battle. However, such was our love for Mary, that the Practice conquered our loquacity and an unaccustomed hush settled on the Convent during May.

We honored Mary as our mother in a special way at Sacred Heart. In the early days of the Society a novice at the Trinita Dei Monte Convent, near the Spanish Steps in Rome, painted a fresco of Mary called *Mater Admirabilis*. This painting was to become an inspiration to generations of Religious and children of the Sacred Heart. It portrayed Mary as a lovely young woman wearing a rose-colored gown and creamy veil. She was serenely seated, as if in meditation, with a spindle at her left hand and a lily at her right. At her feet was a work basket and, on it, an open book. This portrait, reproduced in every Convent of the Sacred Heart, was a visible sermon that showed us how to imitate our Blessed Mother. The lily spoke to us of purity, the spindle and basket of duty and of work and the open book of study and of prayer.

Christmas at the convent began on the first Monday of Advent with the placing of a nativity scene at the front of each study hall. The scene was always the same---a *papier mâché* mountain banked with evergreens, sprinkled with soapflake snow and surmounted by a wooden stable people with statues of the Holy Family. The mountain was terraced in shallow steps and at its base was a flock of small wooden lambs. Each lamb represented one of us and was so identified by a tiny nametag.

By keeping the Advent Practice as we should each day, we enabled the mistress of study hall to move our lambs one step up the mountain. If we were kind, courteous, thoughtful, helpful, or whatever the practice of the day happened to be, our lamb would climb the mountain, step by step, and arrive at the stable on the last day of school before the Christmas holidays. This practice was our birthday gift to the Christ Child, and a very special gift it was, for it was the giving of ourselves.

Each year just before the holidays there was a celebration at which the archbishop, resplendent in scarlet robes, was the honored guest. For this gala event, popularly referred to as the Baskets, the assembly room was radiant with holly wreaths, poinsettias, snow-flocked Christmas trees and the entire student body, bright and beaming in white uniforms. On the floor beside each one of us was a gaily decorated cardboard box, for such, in reality, were the baskets, filled to overflowing with all the necessary ingredients for a delectable Christmas dinner. Our own proud creations, these baskets were another gift to Jesus, a gift later given in His name to the poor.

The culmination of the Christmas festivities was the presentation of our baskets to the Christ Child. For this we carried the baskets, big girls helping little ones, up to the manger on the stage. During this lively promenade we sang countless verses of "Adeste Fidelis" and, without dropping a basket or a beat, curtsied as we passed before the archbishop.

A tableau of the nativity scene was a beautiful and inspiring feature of the Baskets. Filled with the Christmas spirit, those involved always tried to make it as authentic and as perfect as they could. However, I remember a time when the reach for authenticity unwittingly disrupted the striving for perfection. The year I took the part of Mary in the tableau, the nun in charge conceived the horrendous, to me, idea of using a real baby instead of a doll to portray the Infant Jesus. As it turned out my forebodings were justified. For the baby, not realizing that he should exude serenity, screamed into my ringing ears throughout the endless scene. Yet, afterwards, the consensus of opinion, except for mine and possibly the baby's, was one of delighted approbation for this unusual performance.

The Religious of the Sacred Heart were first-rate teachers. Not only were they experts at stretching minds and firing imaginations but also at creating a desire for knowledge where absolutely none existed. At times, however, these dedicated women worked in mysterious ways their wonders to perform. Our second Academic Latin teacher was a case in point. Because of her ingenuity, we found ourselves memorializing a day which, although Roman, was far from being Catholic. This innovative nun was a great fan of Julius Ceasar and all but lived his saga as it unfolded in Latin II. A week or so before the Ides of March, she began to regard us fiercely over rimless, half-moon glasses, and while rapping on her desk, to implore us in sepulchral tones to "Beware the Ides of March." Our attention thus riveted, we approached the awesome day with burning curiosity. Indeed, we applied ourselves to Latin as we never had before. Yet when March fifteen arrived the black-draped classroom and other signs of mourning for the great Ceasar's demise had less power to astonish us than the slight, but unmistakably triumphant smile upon our teacher's face.

The nuns not only had an uncanny ability for leading us academically but also for developing our latent virtues and weeding out our not-so-latent vices. Day by day they sowed the seeds of virtue in our rebellious little souls. Moreover, they were at pains to give us insight into the meaning and the purpose of their efforts. Once a week the Mistress General met with the children of each study hall to define and crystallize the training we received. At this session, called General Instruction, the myriad facets of Sacred Heart education were brought together to give us a clear vision of moral and spiritual values that would forever stand us in good stead.

As we sat ramrod straight behind our desks---no knees crossed, please---manners were translated into morals, meaning into respect for others as well as for ourselves; discipline, into self-discipline; and religion, into the fabric of our lives. A large order, to be sure, but one by which green girls were eventually transformed into a reasonable facsimile of the ideal the Religious had in mind for them.

It would be impossible to write about Sacred Heart education without mentioning a small hinged, hollowed-out wooden instrument that looked like a miniature prayer book but was actually a clapper or signal. Held between the thumb and little finger it could be clicked like a castanet. A nun had only to reach into the pocket of her habit to produce this most effective medium of communication. The Religious used it to capture our attention, to ask for silence, to shape up the ranks and so on. We recognized and responded to the sound of the signal immediately. Harried surveillantes and class mistresses found it an invaluable aid to discipline and also to the human voice. There was never a need for vocal histrionics on the part of the nuns, for the signal was the voice of their authority.

The ringing of bells was the voice of the convent itself. Small melodious golden bells were rung at Mass and Benediction; the tower bell pealed the Angelus; and the clanging of a big brass hand bell proclaimed the hours of the school day.

Our own voices were often raised in song. We sang for Mass, Benediction, feast days, *congés,* and sometimes just for the fun of it. But the loveliest singing of all was that of the nuns chanting the Office. On the rare occasions when we stayed late after school we could hear the clear, liquid notes of this hauntingly beautiful prayer drifting from the direction of the Chapel. The Office was made up of the Psalms. It was the official prayer of the Church and, as such, transcended private prayer. Yet our confidence in those who sang it was so great that we assumed we were remembered in its dulcet tones; for the nuns, in the true manner of mothers, remembered us in all things. They loved us and we knew it. After God, to Whom they strove to bring us, we were their main concern.

Getting Culture

It seems to me when I was growing up that life was one long series of improvement projects, all aimed at the getting of "culture." For us they were "lessons," piano lessons, singing lessons, elocution lessons, dancing lessons, French lessons---whatever was popular at the time or accessible via a nearby teacher.

Everyone in my neighborhood took singing lessons from Miss Hobbs, who later married and as Mrs. Peterson became supervisor of Choral and Classroom Music for the Orleans Parish Public Schools. We took speech lessons from Miss Hastings and French from old Miss Reinecke and piano lessons from Mrs. Jennie Bevinetto Murphy whose family owned the corner grocery store. Most of these teachers lived nearby and we walked to their houses for our lessons, except for "Miss" Jennie who came to our house to give us our piano lessons. The only time we strayed from our own neighborhood for lessons was when we took dancing from Josie Cobera, whose dance studio was uptown on Third Street off St. Charles Avenue.

Some lessons were shortlived. Benny lasted through one elocution class and one guitar lesson. Others went on for years and later became springboards for serious and enjoyable study.

I think now that the craze for all those lessons, aimed ostensibly at developing our natural talents and making us well-rounded individuals, actually had a lot to do with Shirley Temple. This precocious idol of the movies, along with other young stars like Deanna Durbin, Jane Withers, Ann Shirley, and Judy Garland, were the inspiration for many a child and for many a mother. At dancing lessons we were always hearing mothers make remarks like, "Doesn't she looked just like Shirley Temple?" or "Shirley Temple can't dance any better than my daughter," and at singing lessons, it was, "With a little more training, she'll sound just like Deanna Durbin." The movies were a potent and pervading influence and the possibility of being "discovered" and winding up in Hollywood was the common daydream of girls growing up in that era. Who knew when a talent scout might be listening to Professor Schramm's radio program, or might pop into Miss Cobera's Dance Review, or happen to attend Amateur Night at the Bell Show?

All of these were showcases for displaying our "talent" and proving that all those lessons were worth something. They were also the carrot on the stick to keep us going. Every series of classes had its annual or semi-annual recital, review or demonstration of some kind. The grandest was probably the dance review, although singing on the radio was surely one of the most exhilarating experiences of our "cultural" repertoire.

Preparations for the dance review began months before the event itself. Besides learning all the dance routines, there were all those costumes to be made. If you took ballet as well as tap dancing (and acrobatics besides, as I did) you needed at least three different costumes. Mom kept a hot sewing machine with both Helen and me in dancing school. The ordinary dancing lessons themselves required lots of equipment. Our round dance cases were filled with toe shoes, ballet slippers, tap shoes, leotards, tights, lamb's wool (to stuff in toe shoes to ease the pain), head bands (to keep hair out of our eyes) and a towel (we worked up a pretty good sweat, especially in pre-air-conditioned summers.) We took all of these things with us to rehearsals at the Jerusalem Temple, one of the favorite places for dance reviews. We had several rehearsals there before the big night and they, more than the review itself, were the most fun for me. Rehearsals were all-day affairs and in order to keep us amused while we waited our turn on stage, we were allowed to roam about the vast auditorium (it seemed vast then), running up and down the steps and in and out of the aisles. It was one of the few times my mother allowed us to munch uninterruptedly on potato chips, peanuts, and candy. The most delectable treats, however, were the ham sandwiches from the drugstore down the street. Whenever I think of a dance review I get a mental image of myself curled up in an auditorium seat devouring a ham on toast with lettuce, tomato, and mayonnaise.

The dance review was exciting---not enjoyable, but exciting. I was so worried about falling down in the middle of a *tour jeté* or bumping into one

of the other dancers that I couldn't really enjoy it. And we had to keep remembering to smile when our faces all settled into natural frowns from con-
centrating so hard on not making a mistake. No matter how ludicrous we
must have been, we always received thunderous applause (which almost drowned
out the spontaneous laughter). I never advanced enough to warrant a solo
performance, but Helen (two years younger than I) did, and her first solo
turned out to be a showstopper. She was only six years old and a very precocious little dancer she turned out to be. Her solo was a Russian folk dance
which ended with the well-known cossack step, executed while squatting with
arms akimbo and legs thrust forward and back in rapid fire. We had all (including Mother) been practicing this step at home to see who could do it the
longest without losing balance. Helen was the undisputed champ; she could
keep it up for hours. However, she was only supposed to do it ten times at
the conclusion of her number. That night she performed so spiritedly that
after about five cossack steps the audience began applauding. When Helen
heard that applause, it was just too much for her. She kept right on going,
five, ten, fifteen, twenty, much to the consternation of her piano accompanist
and the amusement of the audience. As long as the applause and the laughter
continued, she continued. I guess she would have kept it up the entire night,
cancelling out all other performances, if Miss Cobera had not smilingly but
firmly walked on stage finally and escorted her off. Not a bit fazed, I remember
her waving jauntily to the audience as she and her teacher disappeared into
the wings.

For some reason our singing debut on the radio was even more frightening than the dance review. Perhaps we realized that we were dancing before an audience of family and friends (and any talent scouts that might be
lurking on the premises), but we would be singing for thousands of perfect
strangers out there in radioland. The whole *raison d'être* for the singing lessons, as far as we were concerned, was to demonstrate our vocal talent over
the airways. The most well-known singing studio in town was that of Professor Joseph C. Schramm, who had his own radio program, so all of his pupils
were assured of a radio spot. Other singing teachers, I presume, had to make
their own arrangements with the disc jockeys of the day. At any rate, our
teacher Miss Hobbs was able to arrange one or two radio appearances for us
each year. She took us to the studio in groups of six or seven and we had
a short practice session before going on the air. The first time we broadcast
we were terrified. We had to be absolutely quiet. The microphone was a mys-

terious and somewhat sinister instrument. A strange man (the announcer) asked us questions and tried to make us relax. Fat chance! We were lucky we could remember our own names not to mention the lyrics of the songs we were to sing. None of us was more than eight years old. I remember the questions, "And what is your name, honey?" and "How old are you?" and "What is your selection today?" All were answered in hoarse and trembling voice. The first time I went, I sang "Red Sails in the Sunset." Helen sang "It Looks Like Rain in Cherry Blossom Lane." When we got home from the studio, Benny was still rolling around on the floor, convulsed with laughter. At the time I simply chalked it up to his usual big-brother behavior. Later when I was a young adult I found myself tuning into Professor Schramm's radio program whenever I felt like a really good laugh.

The piano recital wasn't nearly as much fun for Benny as the radio performance. He was, as usual, a member of the audience and not a performer. It wasn't much fun for me either. It lacked the glamour of the dance review and the excitement of the radio appearance. For Benny the recital meant getting all dressed up in a suit and tie and having to listen to me play the piano (and to lots of other boys and girls too) without giving vent to raucous laughter or loud complaints, his usual reaction to my playing. The most he could get away with was some squirming and yawning. When he could not refrain from an occasional giggle, my mother squelched him with a sharp pinch on the arm. That was her favorite way to keep us in line when we were out of line in public.

As for me, to say piano recitals were not much fun is an understatement. I guess I really hated them. The first one wasn't so bad because I didn't know what to expect, and I was at the height of my artistic enthusiasm. I had completed about six months of lessons and enjoyed every one of them. "Miss" Jennie gave me an easy piece, a simplified version of "Liebestraum" and I sailed through it, receiving what I considered at the time to be wild applause from the somewhat sedate audience. After that it was all downhill. The following year and the year after that, the pieces were harder ("March Militaire" and "Claire de Lune"), the practice sessions long and tedious, the performance mediocre and the applause perfunctory. Much to "Miss" Jennie's chagrin, I refused to participate in any more recitals, and after that, piano lessons were fun again.

Elocution lessons were a lot like school, therefore not very popular. Our teacher had a strange accent (she must have been a native of Uptown), and she spent a lot of time trying to combat our Seventh Ward way of speaking. She tried to get us to correctly distinguish our pronunciation of "oi" (as in oyster not "erster") and our "ir" (as in bird, not "boid"). She seemed to have a fixation about our pronunciation of "leg" ("laig") and made up a rhyme for us to practice: "The *bird* laid an *egg* while standing on her *leg*." We also repeated ad infinitum "oy as in boy, oyster, boyster, oyster, boyster." For a long time I thought a "boyster" was a male oyster. After a while I think Miss Hastings became discouraged. She started emphasizing the importance of breathing properly and standing up straight. We walked around with books on our heads while "rounding" our vowels and enunciating our consonants. That, at least, was more fun than "oyster, boyster, oyster, boyster."

As a result of taking two years of French lessons I can still count to twenty in French and can sing the "Marseillaise" from beginning to end. I was very fond of that rousing anthem and two or three of us from the French class thought we sang it so well we considered entering ourselves in Amateur Night at the Bell Show. When my mother heard of this plan she immediately put the "kabosh" on it. Not that we didn't sing the "Marseillaise" very well, she carefully explained, but Amateur Night was not the place to display our expertise. It was not "dignified." She was right. Amateur Night was not dignified, but it was great fun.

Movie theaters in those days had all sorts of gimmicks to attract patrons. They gave away dishes, dictionaries, encyclopedias, and towels. On "Bank Night" they gave away money. But my favorite, and the favorite of every kid in the neighborhood, was Amateur Night. As a small child, I took it very seriously and admired those intrepid souls who got up and performed on the Bell stage in front of all those people. As I got older, I appreciated the humor of Amateur Night which attracted a variety of daring and inventive performers. There were lots of instrumentalists: trumpet players, clarinetists, trombonists, drummers and flute players. Accordion players probably outnumbered them all. *Every* Amateur Night had at least one accordion player. There were ambitious vocalists who tried to sound (and look) like Shirley Temple and Deanna Durbin. There were tons of tap dancers, all trying to be Fred Astaire or Ruby Keeler. There were jugglers, yodelers, bird imitators, orators, magicians, ballet dancers, and dog trainers. The ones that intrigued me the most were the adagio dancers and the contortionists, especially the latter. There was one little girl with black curly hair who could tie herself up just like a pretzel. She wound up her act with her stomach on the floor of the stage, her feet tucked under her chin and her arms stretched out like wings. She entered Amateur Night several times and I would stand up in my seat, look right in her face and wave to her. She'd smile back at me. She never did win first prize, no matter how hard I clapped for her. I don't know what first prize was; maybe they just performed for the glory of it all. Henry Dupré, who later became a well-known New Orleans radio and television personality, was the master of ceremonies. He was friendly and funny and everyone liked him. He introduced the performers and occasionally had the unhappy chore of escorting one off the stage if the situation got unbearable enough. Like the night one little girl, all dressed up in a sailor dress and hat and ready to sing "On the Good Ship Lollipop" got an acute case of stage fright and remained absolutely motionless and speechless staring straight ahead at the audience until Henry mercifully led her away.

There was a special excitement about Amateur Night whenever one of the neighborhood kids was foolhardy enough to enter. Word spread like wildfire and everyone showed up to either clap or jeer. If it was a popular boy or girl, no matter how pitiful the performance, he or she got our tumultuous support. If it was someone unpopular, laughter and cat calls would drive them from the stage in ignominious humiliation. Children can be cruel. There was one boy I remember particularly well who played the trumpet. He practiced every afternoon and Benny and his friends shouted things like "Put a nickel in it" when they passed his house. He got the same kind of treatment when he was on the stage trying to blow his way through "Pennies from Heaven," an unfortunate selection. The boys started throwing pennies onto the stage amid guffaws and whistles until Mr. Shields, the manager of the theater, made an appearance and escorted them from the premises.

I doubt if anyone who appeared on the Bell Show stage for Amateur Night ever had a career as a professional performer (except for Henry Dupré) but I bet they all remember their night in the limelight, and so do we who sat in the audience.

Of course we would have gone to the movies even if there had never been an Amateur Night. For the movies were an exciting, important, almost dominant part of our lives. Just as children today find it hard to imagine living without television, I would have found it hard to imagine living without the movies. Margaret and her friends experienced this same celluloid magic.

The Movies

The shimmer of the silver screen brightened the landscape of the thread-bare thirties and, along with Technicolor's peacock palette, camouflaged the grim years of World War II. Those were the days when the movies stood for the sheer joy of escape. Troubles were checked at the box-office and theatres were entered in the hope of living vicariously, at least for an hour or so, in a carefree, glamorous world. Young people, especially, immersed themselves in Hollywood's tinsel trappings, sighing over celluloid heroes and heroines long after the last reel was run.

In downtown New Orleans, as in all big cities, the theatres themselves were opulent avenues of escape. Architecturally grand and unabashedly pretentious, their design was predominately rococo. Upon stepping into the lobby of one of these motion-picture palaces, the moviegoer was plunged into a world of gilded grandeur. The typical theatre lobby was an Alladin's cave of gleaming gold leaf, soaring pillars and voluptuous statuary. This baroque environment was cleverly designed to set the stage for a smooth passage from the mundane world to the never-never land of the movies.

Of all the movie theatres downtown, the Saenger and the Loew's State on Canal Street and the Orpheum just around the corner on University Place, were the largest and most glittering. The Loew's State and the Orpheum were gilded beauties designed in the lavish style of European opera houses. The Saenger, however, was unique. Called an "atmospheric" theatre, its auditorium resembled a large outdoor square overlooked by Renaissance palaces and, even more amazing, its ceiling simulated a night sky of twinkling stars and floating clouds.

During those days of cinema flamboyance these palatial theatres were the focus of an exciting rite of female passage into adolescence. This ritual took place when parents at long last allowed their daughters to attend the Saturday matinee unchaperoned. Unchaperoned meaning in the company of at least one other girl but never, God forbid, alone.

In preparation for our maiden voyage we, the happy initiates, primped, preened, and dressed up to the nines. This meant wearing our very best dresses, purses, hats, and even gloves---short, white, cotton gloves in warm weather and dark gloves that matched our accessories in the winter. Then, our toilettes complete, we swayed and rattled downtown via streetcar, in my case, the St. Charles Avenue streetcar. Along the way a metamorphosis took place, for when we reached Canal Street we were no longer callow school girls but sophisticated women of the world. Or so we liked to think.

Our first stop was the drugstore, Katz and Besthoff (better known as K & B) on the corner of Canal and Dauphine Streets. It was the current rage. To our wide-eyed naiveté this establishment was unrivalled by any restaurant in town, including such renowned gourmet temples as Arnaud's, Antoine's and Galatoire's. Its luncheon menu was a gastronomic treat. There was no mention of a carrot, a dish of spinach or any other vegetable on it. Except for sandwiches and soft drinks it was a treasure trove of sweets.

As we scanned the list of sundaes, sodas, multi-flavored ice creams and assorted *à la modes*, it dawned on us that, free of adult supervision, we could order as we pleased. In view of this, a banana split and a soda seemed to be the perfect lunch.

But we were doomed to disappointment. One furtive glance around the room convinced us that this combination would be a social gaffe. The fashionable lunch was, obviously, a sandwich, a sundae and a cherry coke. So this was what we ordered---conformity winning hands down over independence.

As luck would have it, we were pleasantly surprised. Indeed, our mandatory meal was such a treat that---forgetting plans to nibble daintily---we finished in our usual record time. But before leaving for the show we retrieved our new found *savoir faire*. We tipped the long-suffering waitress, dabbed pale orange lipstick on our baby faces and wished, alas in vain, for the nerve to smoke a cigarette.

The idea of watching a movie minus candy was unthinkable. Once past the box office we made a beeline for the candy stand. Then, clutching candy bars and popcorn, we stepped into the splendor of the lobby. To enter that rarefied atmosphere was to come excitingly close to the rainbow's end. I, for one, would not have been surprised to see the likes of Greta Garbo or Clark Gable pop out from behind a potted palm.

Our arrival at the show never seemed to coincide with the beginning of the feature film. So, on groping our way into the pitch-black inner sanctum of the theatre, we were due for a surprise. There was no way of knowing if we would come in during the newsreel, the comedy, or the feature film itself. If the feature film was playing, we had to concentrate immediately on the plot. But once its mysteries were unravelled, we tossed reality to the winds and plunged into the action on the screen.

In that heady brew we underwent a startling change. Our wildest dreams came true. We sang like nightingales, danced divinely, clowned with mad abandon and rose to dizzying, dramatic heights. But, best of all, we were irresistible to men. Exuding sex-appeal and glamour, we were wooed and won by every leading man we saw.

Fortunately, we enjoyed our femme fatale-hood to the hilt downtown, for the neighborhood theatres had no room for such a breed. Open every night and on Sunday afternoon, they were attended by our elders on Saturday night and weeknights, but on Friday night and Sunday afternoon they were strictly our domain.

At the matinee on Sunday, following church and Sunday dinner, we were all dressed up and on our best behavior, but on Friday nights we howled. Friday night was serial night. There was a feature film, but the serial was the main attraction. A wild and wooly thriller, it ended in a blazing burst of turbulence, at which point, when we were frantic with excitement, the words "To Be Continued" appeared upon the screen.

The boys in the audience participated vociferously in the serial, especially when it was a western. As gunfire, hoofbeats, and barroom brawls exploded from the screen they whistled, shouted, booed, and stamped their feet until the theatre shook. While this pandemonium reigned, the usherettes, ladies of a certain age who had the job of vigilantes, patrolled the aisles. They scurried back and forth with darting flashlights, trying vainly to restore the peace. We girls enjoyed the serial, but the feature film was more our cup of tea. Especially its romantic moments. The boys, however, scorned such tender sentiment, or, as they called it, mush, and made rude noises and derogatory comments throughout the love scenes. This put a damper on our flights of fancy and made it difficult, if not impossible, to reach the shores of Camelot that welcomed us downtown.

We held no grudge, however. For, although the boys had come to see the serial, we had come to see the boys. During the short subjects, the comedy, the travelogue, the newsreel and so on, we held whispered conferences on the presence, and if present and accounted for, the whereabouts of our current crushes. Then, with fluttering pulses and a budding battery of wiles, we left out seats to stalk our prey.

On one pretence or another---the candy stand, the powder room, the water cooler---we wandered up and down aisles. The usherettes, alert as always, kept an eagle eye on us. Probing the darkness with their flashlights, they popped up like jacks-in-the-box wherever we happened to be. The theatre was perpetual motion, for the boys were also on the move, legitimately heading for our pseudo goals while blissfully oblivious to us. When the short subjects were over, we all settled down again---a phenomenon for which the harried usherettes undoubtedly gave thanks.

The boys were great fans of cowboy movies starring Gene Autry and Johnny Mack Brown and of gangster movies starring Edward G. Robinson and James Cagney. But we girls loved the comedies, musicals and historical extravaganzas that brimmed with gorgeous settings, striking clothes, happy endings and romantic plots. The heroes of these movies were always handsome and the heroines beautiful. We identified completely with the heroines and also with the stars who played them. Indeed, we imitated the stars for all we were worth. Garbo's pageboy hairdo, Joan Crawford's full red lips, Dietrich's sucked in cheeks and almost every female star's plucked eyebrows were grist for our mill. Platinum blonde hair was also a great enticement but one at which we, of necessity, stopped short.

We sang tunes from the movies and read the books their plots were based on. In fact, the movies were my introduction to *Wuthering Heights, Romeo and Juliet, Gone With the Wind* and *A Midsummer Night's Dream.* In many families---and certainly in mine---the approval of the Hays Office, with its rigid production code, and the Legion of Decency of the Catholic Church were required before children and young people were allowed to go to the show. Most movies were acceptable, however, for sex on the screen was non-existent, bad language was banned and violence was minimal.

With the onset of World War II, the escapist films of the Depression gave way to war movies that inspired patriotism and support of the war effort. Romance remained intact, however, in the wartime films, for there was always a boy-girl element to their plots. As far as we girls were concerned, favorites such as Van Johnson and Robert Taylor were inbued with added glamour when---more handsome than ever in uniform---they gallantly coped with the tragedies and stresses of war. The newsreels, however, gave us an unnerving glimpse of the war as it really was.

When we went to the movies we were assured of a tempting smorgasbord of entertainment. In addition to the feature film---which was, occasionally a double feature--we were treated to a short subject such as The Our Gang Comedy or a cartoon featuring the likes of Donald Duck or Bugs Bunny. We could also be sure of seeing a newsreel as well as film clips from coming productions and, sometimes, a travelogue took us on a journey to exotic places. And on Friday nights the serial was an added bonus.

Movie stars were very real to us. Having seen them so often on the screen, we felt we knew them well, yet we had a strong desire to know them even better. Movie magazines fulfilled that need. Teeming with information, they made the lives, loves, homes and swimming pools of the stars an open book.

We girls devoured the magazines, but the boys regarded them with scorn. Although they were never ripe with purple prose or photographs, our parents sometimes banned them, telling us what fine students we would be if we gave the same attention to our studies that we gave to movie stars.

But, *semper fidelis* to our idols, we continued to research their lifestyles, reading the magazines over and over again. Then, having extracted every ounce of stellar information from their pages, we reduced them to shreds by cutting out the pictures of the biggest, brightest stars. We pasted the pictures of our favorites in scrapbooks and saved the rest for trading with our friends.

Trading was a serious enterprise that taught us how to wheel and deal and hold out for the highest bidder. A few brave souls actually wrote to Hollywood requesting autographed photographs of the stars. When traded on the open market these photographs were worth their weight in gold. Come to think of it, with memorabilia on the rise, they should be worth their weight in gold today. But, alas, we lacked a crystal ball to see the future, and our pictures are long gone.

Holy Days and Holidays

After a trip to Mexico City a few years ago a Yankee friend of mine told me of seeing devout Mexicans walking on their knees for several blocks to approach the Shrine of Our Lady of Guadalupe. She was obviously fascinated and at the same time mildly repelled by what she considered a primitive and superstitious practice. I somewhat sheepishly confessed that I had several times in my youth climbed on my knees up the steps of St. Ann's Shrine on Ursulines Avenue right here in New Orleans.

"You've got to be kidding! Whatever for?" was her spontaneous response.

"Whatever for?" Thinking about it, I decided that I had climbed the steps on my knees because my friends and lots of other people were doing it. It was a special penitential practice we followed for Good Friday. I say "penitential" although it had the same air of celebration as "making" the nine churches, another of our Good Friday customs (which I'll explain later).

In New Orleans holy days and holidays used to be, as in their ancient origin, the same thing. Because of the Catholic Southern European culture of New Orleans, religious observances were an important part of our year. Even Mardi Gras, that seemingly pagan extravaganza, was (and still is) the city's last fling before its solemn religious observance of Lent. Many consider New Orleans the most Catholic city in the United States, not because it has more Catholics than any other city, but because Catholicism has influenced the city's culture so much. There may be more Catholics in Boston than in New Orleans, but Boston could hardly be described as a Catholic city. On the other hand, any newcomer to New Orleans can immediately recognize the unmistakably Catholic ambience which New Orleanians, no matter what their religion, simply take for granted. When I was in seventh grade at Mc-

Donogh Number 28 Public School, our history teacher asked the class what was the predominant religion of the United States. Everyone, Catholic and non-Catholic alike, replied in unison "Catholic!" The teacher smiled and said "Every class gives the same answer." We were all astonished when she informed us that Catholics were in the minority in most parts of our country.

Unlike Catholics in many other places, New Orleans Catholics are comfortable and unself-conscious about their religion and some of the unique ways in which they observe it. The non-Catholics of New Orleans readily accept a heritage that makes room for King Cakes and baby dolls (part of the Twelfth Night celebration), lucky fava beans (given away on St. Joseph Day), novenas, and treks to nine churches (a Good Friday practice). In the days when the Catholic Church observed meatless Fridays as a penance, Catholics in some places were dubbed "mackerel snappers." In New Orleans Fridays simply became a traditional day for everyone, Catholic or not, to enjoy seafood gumbo, oyster loaves, boiled crabs, shrimp creole, crawfish étouffé, turtle stew, and other seafood delicacies.

New Orleanians have a way of turning almost anything, even penance, into something enjoyable. That must be why I always think of Lent as a time of both deprivation and celebration. Almost every religious observance felt like a holiday to me when I was a child, even Good Friday. For one thing, we did literally have a holiday from school on many holy days, whether we went to public or Catholic school, so we were all well disposed to celebrate them, either solemnly or joyously. Some holy days, like All Saints' Day and Good Friday, are no longer observed with the fervor and color I remember when growing up.

All Saints' Day on November first was one of my favorites, perhaps because it was our first holiday after school started in September. Halloween, of course, was the night before All Saints' Day and it was always especially exciting because we knew we had no school the next day. We didn't trick or treat in those days. We had neighborhood parties with dunking for apples, scavenger hunts and games of hide and seek.

No matter what the weather was like on Halloween, All Saint's Day was always glorious---cool and brilliantly sunny year after year. In the Catholic Church, All Saints' Day is a special day of the year for remembering the dead, particularly the saints, all the people who have died and are now with God, not just official saints who have their own special feast day in the Church's calendar. It has always been the custom in New Orleans to visit the graves of our loved ones on this day, decorating them with big bunches of flowers, especially chrysanthemums. Florists in New Orleans have their biggest sales of the year on All Saints' Day.

In our family we got up early to attend seven o'clock Mass so we could make the day as long as possible. When we came out of church, vendors were selling big chrysanthemums and I longed for my mother to buy a bunch of those long-stemmed fluffs of white and yellow, but we always walked briskly by as I cast covetous eyes on the vendors' colorful bouquets. My mother took some roses from her garden instead. After a big breakfast, my brother Benny, my sister Helen and I waited impatiently for my mother to gather her supplies together---a broom, a watering can, a thermos of chocolate milk and a bag of cookies.   At about 9:30 we set off on foot for St. Louis Cemetery Number 3, with a few neighborhood friends tagging along with us. We walked from our house on Gentilly Boulevard to Esplanade Avenue and out Esplanade toward Bayou St. John. The cemetery was on Esplanade just a couple of blocks from the Bayou, about a mile from our house. We took turns carrying the supplies, running ahead and then back, seeing people we knew along the way and occasionally picking a flower from someone's garden and telling my mother we found it on the sidewalk. She considered flower stealing a grave crime, but on All Saints' Day she accepted our fib with a smile and added the booty to her bouquet. The cemetery was one of our favorite places to play on our walks to City Park, but today our visit was purposeful.

Tourists flock to see New Orleans cemeteries because of their imposing monuments and ornamented tombs all neatly lined up along wide, criss-crossing avenues. "Cities of the Dead" they call them. Any tourist who might have happened by on All Saints' Day when we were children would have found that usually apt description singularly out of place. When we passed through the great wrought iron gates of St. Louis Number 3, we found the whole cemetery noisily and busily alive with families sweeping out tombs, filling granite and marble vases with water, arranging flowers, and occasionally praying. We were soon doing the same things at the grave of my mother's grandmother. Unlike most of the tombs in St. Louis Number 3, which are like marble houses topped by ornate crosses or statues, my great-grandmother's burial place was a simple underground grave with a granite apron and headstone, located near the back of the cemetery. My mother immediately set to work sweeping and weeding and sent us off to fill the flower vases with water from a nearby faucet, a task we managed to accomplish while spraying each other thoroughly. After we had cleaned the grave and arranged the flowers in the vases, we all knelt on the granite apron at the foot of the grave (I'll never forget how hard that granite was), and my mother led us in saying the rosary. There was much squirming and scratching and yawning, but we tolerated the praying pretty well because we knew that playtime was at the end of the last amen. When that was said—with much gusto—we jumped up and as soon as circulation had returned to our legs we were off and running. We didn't know or care that St. Louis Number 3 is one of the city's most notable cemeteries. It was planned after one of New Orleans' many epidemics of yellow fever and was consecrated in 1854. It has a memorial monument to the city's famous architect, James Gallier, Sr., who was drowned in a shipwreck in 1866. For us, the cemetery was an exciting playground. We ran up and down the aisles, in and out among the tombs, and jumped out at each other with ferocious expressions. Other children were doing the same thing and we sometimes teamed up with another group to play hide and seek. The grown-ups didn't seem to mind all this revelry as long as we didn't interfere with their chores or upset any flower vases. After about an hour we drifted back to my mother, waiting patiently under her perpetual parasol with thermos and cookies in hand. Fortified with these refreshments, we paused for one more quick prayer for all the souls in purgatory and then headed for home, not quite so exuberantly as we'd set out that morning, but pleasantly satisfied with the day's activities.

Next to All Saints' Day, my own favorite day for religious expression was Good Friday. I think I realized the religious significance of Christmas and Easter when I was a child, but the spiritual fervor of those holy days was diluted with the prospect of presents and new clothes. But Good Friday! One couldn't fail to understand what that was all about. The whole day was devoted to recalling the suffering of Christ and in some way trying to share a bit of it. Good Friday was the dramatic highlight of the 40 days of Lent, the penitential season which began on Ash Wednesday, the day after Mardi Gras. It was the culmination of our Lenten sacrificial program; a program we began planning even before Lent began. Occasionally, preparations for Mardi Gras were interrupted by thoughts of what we were going to give up for Lent. Lent and Good Friday were serious business. In school we compared notes with friends about what they were planning to give up: usually treats like candy, cookies, gum, Barq's (a favorite local soft drink), or whatever. At home and in school we heard lectures about practicing patience and charity, and were encouraged to do good deeds, in secret if possible.

Ash Wednesday came with a sobering crunch after those final whirlwind days of Mardi Gras madness. Ash Wednesday was no holiday. We were wakened early, no matter how exhausted we were from the revelry of Mardi Gras Day, and shepherded to early Mass where the priest marked our foreheads with ashes. To me Lent always began when I heard the priest say the words, "Dust thou art, and unto dust thou shalt return." That jolted me into a properly solemn frame of mind and I went off to school determined to carry out all those resolutions and sacrificial practices for the next 40 days of Lent. During that seemingly interminable time until the arrival of Easter, we compared notes with our friends on the success or failure of our attempts at sacrifice and discussed various strategies for the celebration of Good Friday. My Protestant friends were equally earnest about their Lenten sacrifices. A Greek Orthodox friend of mine often attended the Way of the Cross with me on Friday evenings during Lent and a Methodist friend tagged along when we made the nine churches on Good Friday. Visiting nine churches on foot was the traditional penance for Good Friday and there was much talk during Holy Week about plans and strategies for the day. "Are you making the nine churches this year?" "Which ones did you pick?" "When are you starting out?" I heard the older children in school and in the neighborhood talking about their plans and could hardly wait till I was old enough to embark on such an adventure myself.

I think I was about ten when my mother first let me make the nine churches with a group of boys and girls in my neighborhood, the oldest being about 15 years old. My brother Benny, who was 14, selected the churches after studying a map of New Orleans and working out the most efficient route. Planning was essential since we had to walk the whole way, to and from all nine churches.

I was as excited about that first Good Friday expedition as I was about my first fishing trip and my first excursion to the movies uptown. I would be going to parts of the city I'd never been to before, to churches I'd never seen. Who knew what sights I might find along the way? I looked on it as a great adventure. We woke up early on Good Friday and I knew immediately there was something different about the day, it was so quiet. No radio, no singing, no whistling. We ate a Spartan breakfast---milk and biscuits. And my mother didn't have the usual bag of cookies and sandwiches for us to take on the road either. The mood of Good Friday was somber and austere.

As our group assembled at a neighbor's house and we began our long trek to the nine churches, we spoke quietly and were careful not to laugh or smile. We passed the Bell movie theater on Grand Route St. John and Bayou Road and noticed the billboard covered with black lettering: "Closed: Good Friday." Any inclination to skip or hop between the lines on the pavement was immediately suppressed. If anyone inadvertently began to hum or sing, he or she was quickly frowned into silence by the others. This pious attitude lasted for about three churches. We hit Holy Rosary Church on Esplanade Avenue near St. Louis Cemetery Number 3 first. An air of sorrow and emptiness hung in the silent church. All the statues were covered with purple cloth, symbol of mourning, and the open sanctuary door on the altar revealed that, for this one day of the year, Christ was not present there. We had resolved to pray for five minutes at each church but here we began our journey with the Way of the Cross, pausing at each of the 14 stations for at least 30 seconds. Then we were off to St. Ann's Church and Shrine on Ursulines Avenue. That's where I first saw people climbing the steps of the Shrine on their knees. We considered joining them but decided that with seven more churches to visit we'd better leave that particular penance for another Good Friday. After a brief stop at Sacred Heart on Canal Street we trudged on to Our Lady of Guadalupe on North Rampart and Conti Streets. This is the oldest church building in the city, dating from 1826, and was originally a mortuary chapel for the funerals of yellow-fever victims. We were beginning to feel a little bit like victims ourselves by this time. The fervor of our spiritual journey was beginning to pall. However, we looked in at the Grotto of St. Bernadette of Lourdes at the side of the church and were deeply impressed by the collection of braces and crutches hanging on the walls, eloquent testimony to the rewards of strong and resolute faith. The Grotto was a favorite place of prayer for the sick and lame, many of whom left these mementos of their affliction at the Grotto after their prayers were answered. Heartened by this inspiring sight, we continued on, crossing over Rampart Street to the French Quarter, heading for St. Mary's Italian Church on Chartres Street and the St. Louis Cathedral across from Jackson Square. Our trip through the French Quarter took on the air of a holiday romp as we skipped along, peering into courtyards and studying the contents of antique and novelty shop windows along Royal Street. By the time we reached our final destination, St. Rose of Lima, our parish church on Bayou Road, fatigue and hunger had reinstated in us a suitable demeanor of sorrow and sacrifice. No one had abandoned ship along the way and we all felt a sense of satisfaction at our accomplishment and well prepared for the celebration of Easter.

Preceding the penitential days of Lent and Good Friday were the joyful party days of Carnival, which began with another of my favorite feasts, King's Day or Twelfth Night. This was the Church's Feast of Epiphany on January 6 ---twelve days after Christmas---celebrating the visitation of the Three Wise Men, or Kings, to the Christ Child. In many European countries Epiphany is almost as important as Christmas and is the time for giving gifts. In our neighborhood the day was welcomed as "King Cake Day." We officially ended the Christmas season on that day by taking down our Christmas tree, burning it and having a King Cake party afterward. The King Cake is apparently something unique to New Orleans---at least within the United States. The tradition originated in France and Italy during the Middle Ages and was brought to New Orleans by the early French settlers. The custom was to serve a cake on Epiphany which contained a bean. The lucky person receiving the bean was declared king or queen for the day and was expected to host a party the following week. In New Orleans the cakes are usually baked in an open oval shape and decorated with icing or sugar of purple, gold and green, the colors of Carnival. At some time the bean was replaced by a small china baby doll which has now become a small plastic doll.

The most elegant King Cake party in town is the annual Ball of the Twelfth Night Revelers, one of the most exclusive of the Carnival organizations, established in 1870. The Queen and maids of the ball are selected from a group of debutantes. Each one receives a box from a giant papier mâché King Cake. The lucky girl who receives a gold bean in her box is Queen and those who receive a silver bean are her maids.

Many New Orleanians observe King's Day with a simple King Cake party. When we were little, parties were mostly family affairs; a few relatives or another family came over for cake and coffee. All the kids carefully inspected the cake, selecting portions they felt sure contained the baby doll. At that age, getting the baby was a thrill. My mother always had a homemade crown for the lucky boy or girl who found the baby. As we approached the teenage years, however, King Cake parties took on a new dimension. Our family party became a neighborhood boy-girl party and whoever got the baby at the first party was host or hostess at another party the following Sunday. We kept up the cycle of Sunday parties until Mardi Gras. Getting the baby was then a whole new ballgame. It seemed to me that none of the girls minded getting the baby; in fact, we girls were secretly delighted to have the opportunity to give a party. But the boys had to be watched carefully to see that they didn't slip the baby into their pocket or surreptitiously drop it on the floor. None was desperate or foolhardy enough to swallow the china babies we had in those days. If a boy did get the baby he picked one of the girls to be his queen and if a girl got it, she designated one of the boys as her king. After a couple of parties the choosing of the king or queen became the most anticipated and dramatic point of the evening. It was the source of spirited speculation and sometimes fearful anxiety during the week, at least on the part of the girls. I don't know about the boys. The final King Cake party was the Sunday before Mardi Gras. The lucky one who got the baby was committed to giving the first King Cake party the following year.

Of course the most extravagant and flamboyant of all our holidays, the one holiday we anticipated as enthusiastically as Christmas, was Mardi Gras. Mardi Gras is so much a part of New Orleans culture that we have devoted two separate chapters to it.

The solemnity of the 40 days of Lent was interrupted twice between Ash Wednesday and Easter, the Feast of St. Patrick on March 17 and the Feast of St. Joseph on March 19. St. Patrick's Day was not so exuberantly celebrated then as it is today, at least not in my neighborhood. Everyone wore a green ribbon or tie and my mother cooked corned beef and cabbage, and we felt rather festive. But that was about it.

St. Joseph's Day was something else. Many Italians, especially Sicilians, immigrated to New Orleans and they brought with them the custom of the St. Joseph altar. Their veneration of St. Joseph, the foster father of Jesus, is symbolized by the preparation of huge amounts of food which they display on "altars" dedicated to St. Joseph. After inviting their relatives and neighbors in to see and admire their altar they give the food to the poor. The custom goes back to the Middle Ages when grateful Sicilians credited St. Joseph with saving them from a famine. A bountiful crop of fava beans carried them through the year and the fava bean is today distributed as a lucky charm to those who visit St. Joseph altars. In my neighborhood this feast was a big event because we had several Italian families and two of them competed for the most elaborate St. Joseph altars. As a young child I had the impression that only Italians were invited to view the altars and given a lucky bean and a slice of sesame bread or cookie as a token of hospitality and good fortune. I was always sorry on St. Joseph Day that I could not claim Italian ancestry.

We became good friends with the Bevinetto family that owned the corner grocery store and one year they invited us to their altar. We all thought it a great privilege and dressed up for the occasion, all except my brother Benny who, finding out that we were not allowed to eat any of the food but only admire it and receive a fava bean and a cookie, refused to go. I was very impressed, however, with the opportunity to see so much food collected at one time in one small place.

As we entered the dining room, I was dazzled by the flickering light of candles burning in front of numerous statues, mostly of the Blessed Mother, presiding over tables laden with an extravagant variety and quantity of food. Besides the large dining table and buffet, there were a number of cloth-covered card tables (the grocery was the headquarters for a regular Friday night neighborhood poker game). The heavy aroma of Parmesan cheese, tomatoes, basil, and oregano assailed our nostrils. In the center of the dining table, surrounded and hemmed in by stuffed artichokes and tomatoes, lasagna, stuffed peppers, baked macaroni, boiled shrimp, sesame seed bread and mounds of apples, grapes and pineapples, was a large statue of St. Joseph himself. Mrs. Bevinetto told me she burned a candle in front of this statue every day of the year and never buried her statue in the back yard as the Little Sisters of the Poor did. According to her, when things were going badly for the Convent of the Little Sisters or the nuns needed something, they would pray to St. Joseph and bury a statue of the saint in their yard. Sister Mary Vincent, administrator of the Little Sisters of the Poor, tells me that this custom is no longer followed. When praying for a special intention these days the nuns sometimes place a picture of their desired project or intention in front of a statue of St. Joseph and pray for his intercession. Sister Mary Vincent recounts an amusing true story of how St. Joseph answered the prayers of an old gentleman in their nursing home. It seems that the old man complained of not having enough beer served in the home. He placed a beer can with flowers in front of a statue of St. Joseph and made his petition for more beer. A visiting priest at the home inquired about the unusual flower container in front of St. Joseph's statue and was told of the old man's prayer. Next day the priest was on a plane traveling to another city and started chuckling as he remembered the old man and the beer can. The man sitting next to him asked the cause of his mirth and after the priest told his story, the man said, "You may find this hard to believe, Father, but I own a brewery and if the Little Sisters of the Poor want more beer, they're going to get it." "And we did," said Sister Mary Vincent.

A secular holiday peculiar to New Orleans and one that I remember fondly was McDonogh Day, held on the first Friday of May to honor John McDonogh, the great benefactor of New Orleans public schools. It seemed to me that my friends who attended Catholic schools were always getting extra holidays for some special religious feast. Here at last we public school students at McDonogh Number 28, and other public schools all over town, had a special holiday of our own. Of course, it was only a half holiday because the morning was given over to visiting the statue of John McDonogh in Lafayette Square across from the old City Hall (now Gallier Hall) on St. Charles Avenue and Girod Street. But that was fun. We assembled at school, all carrying bouquets which our mothers had plucked from their gardens that morning. I was always proud of mine because my mother had a prolific and bountiful flower garden. The teachers always noticed the best bouquets and placed their owners in the front of the line. That meant that we got the best seats in the bus and were first to place our flowers at the foot of McDonogh's statue. We sang the "Ode to McDonogh" (to the tune of "Tannenbaum") on our way, filling the bus with strains of "He gave his wealth to *educate*, the boys and girls of Twenty-*eight*," adding a personal lyrical twist of our own. As spirits rose the boys were soon yodeling "He gave his wealth to educate, the stupid girls of Twenty-eight" and the girls were trying loudly to drown them out with their opposite version. As a first grader my impression of McDonogh Day was awe and amazement at the gigantic number of children all assembled in one place, row after row of them marching along, placing flowers at the base of the statue while singing the "Ode to McDonogh." We all felt deeply grateful to our benefactor, but more for the holiday he afforded us, I'm afraid, than the school system he helped to build for us.

Of course Christmas, Easter and New Year's Day were religious celebrations and our spiritual observance was supposed to be pre-eminent. In the case of New Year's, it was not so pre-eminent. But on Christmas, attending Mass was almost as important as awaiting the arrival of Santa Claus. On New Year's Day attending Mass was strictly an obligation (it was a holy day of obligation, the Feast of the Circumcision of Christ). We went, tired and dragging our heels. The big event of the day, besides dinner, was the Sugar Bowl game at the Tulane Stadium uptown on Willow Street. If you weren't lucky enough to have a ticket, you listened to it on the radio, and caught up on your sleep after staying up till midnight to usher in the New Year. Before fireworks were outlawed in New Orleans, the entire city sounded like a battle zone as midnight approached. Sometimes the whine of an ambulance could be heard above the popping of firecrackers, cherry bombs, Roman candles and other assorted fireworks, as some unfortunate pyrotechnician was carted off to the hospital for the treatment of wounds received in the course of the New Year's celebration. My own enthusiasm for fireworks was permanently dampened when a small firecracker exploded in my hand one New Year's Eve. I have a bit of black sulphur embedded in my right palm as a reminder.

Easter had an especially festive air because it meant the end of our Lenten sacrifices. Mass was actually enjoyable, attended by all of us in brand new spring clothes---symbolic, we were told, of the new life Jesus gave us with his resurrection. The rest of the day was spent gorging ourselves on chocolate rabbits and assorted Easter eggs. On more than one occasion, we talked our mother into buying us baby chickens or ducks, usually dyed violent pink or yellow, and always prominently displayed in the local market. Long before they were visible to us, their presence was proclaimed by their strident "peeping", a sound we always found completely captivating. Keeping them alive was a full-time job, and my mother deserves credit for whatever success we had. She saw that the chicks or ducklings were kept warm in a box with an electric light bulb. We actually raised several such Easter "pets" to adulthood and then proudly released them in City Park or gave them to Audubon Zoo for its barnyard enclosure.

Following Easter, holiday time hit a slump. Except for McDonogh Day we didn't celebrate another until July Fourth, which we considered pretty second rate because it occurred during summer, and summer was one big holiday anyway.

Holidays and holy days were big events in our lives. They marked the cycle of the year, they provided zest and sparkle to our lives, and they instilled in us an anticipation and relish for celebration, a quality of childhood that is often dimmed in adult years. New Orleans, more than most places, allows that childhood quality to persist no matter how many cycles of holidays we live through.

Life between our holy days and holidays was filled with a variety of activities and amusements centered in our homes, often on our front porches and around our fireplaces. Margaret remembers some of her growing-up experiences on the porch and by the fire.

Summer on the Porch

Uptown and downtown, in fact all over town, New Orleans was a city of porches. They dominated the scene like a web of cool oases, providing summertime refreshment and almost year-round pleasure. Most houses could boast at least one porch, some houses sprouted them at random and others were completely wreathed by them. But the front porch was the universal favorite.

Our front porch was the delight of my childhood. Sheltered by awnings and shrubs and furnished with old-fashioned rocking chairs, it stretched, long and cool, across the front of our house, a standing invitation to come outside. Beyond its railings we could see the tree-shaded gardens and Victorian houses on our block. In springtime when the azaleas burst into bloom the gardens were a rosy foam, but in summer, fall, and winter they were leafy, sea-green bowers. The street, too, was a bower for it was canopied by the branches of huge oak trees that grew along the sidewalks. This sylvan setting was a perfect foil for the ever-changing kaleidoscope of sights and sounds that passed our house on summer days.

After breakfast my brother and I made a beeline to the porch for a morning of play and street watching. The passing parade began with the deliverymen making their morning rounds. We could always count on seeing the milkman, the mailman, and even the iceman, for our family still preferred the old-time block ice to more up-to-date ice cubes.

Streetcars punctuated the scene now and then, rattling and swaying back and forth between Audubon Park and Canal Street. Brother and I were always on the lookout for a familiar face on board and, sensing this, a friendly conductor often saluted us with a loud clang of his bell. On fine days, an

67

old lady, sitting erect and dignified beneath an unfurled parasol, rode by in a horse-drawn open carriage with a top-hatted coachman at the reins. Another passerby, the Cat Lady, was diametrically opposed to this romantic vision. She strolled by each morning dressed in nightgown and robe and followed by a retinue of snooty feline friends.

Not long after this apparition disappeared, a ramshackle wagon came creaking up the street. Pulled by a melancholy mule wearing a straw bonnet, it listed precariously to one side beneath a load of fruit and vegetables. Its driver was nicknamed "I Got" after the recurring words of his sales pitch. "I got corn, I got okra, I got bananas," he would cry. "I got snapbeans, I got eggplant, I got watermelon red to the rind." Since we were regular customers of "I Got" he would pull over to the curb at our house. This was a signal for Mother and Rosie, our cook, to come out and make their selections for the day. It was also a signal for Brother and me to request a little something to tide us over until lunchtime.

A multitude of peddlers followed in "I Got's" wake. They transformed the street into a mobile market as they hawked their products. Each peddler had a different mode of verbal advertising, but all of their cries had a similarity to the haunting cadences of liturgical plainchant. Some of them sauntered by with baskets of luscious Louisiana strawberries, succulent river shrimp or plump Creole tomatoes slung over their arms or balanced on their heads. Others rumbled by on wagons piled high with bananas just off the boat or watermelons from outlying truck farms. The Waffle Man blew a bugle to herald his arrival and the Taffy Man sounded a gong. The Blackberry Woman peddled her purple berries; the Knife and Scissors Grinder plied his trade, and the Rag Man solicited old rags and bottles. An organ grinder and his monkey provided entertainment, and two roving photographers, one equipped with a pony, the other with a goat and cart, sought subjects for their art.

But of all the peddlers the Fig Woman was our favorite. Young as we were we realized she had that certain something called star quality. Long before we saw her we could hear her plaintive chant. "Fresh figs, fresh figs, who'll buy my fresh figs?" she cried. We, of course, had every intention of buying her figs. After a quick trip inside for a container to hold them and small change for their purchase, we hurried back to the porch. Gradually the volume of the peddler's cry increased until at last she herself appeared, a tall, buxom Negress in a long gingham dress and a voluminous white apron. She was as stately and regal as a tribal queen as she made her way along the sidewalk balancing the basket of figs upon her head. This acrobatic feat never failed to impress us and, although impatient for a taste of her fruit, we always made proper obeisance to her queenly carriage and athletic skill. In other words, we minded our manners and for this phenomenon we were invariably rewarded with a dazzling smile and an extra handful of figs.

Running a close second to the Fig Woman was the Snowball Man. This popular vendor pushed a white cart festooned with jingling bells and bottles of jewel-toned flavorings. During the long, steaming summers, nothing was more refreshing than a snowball. Served in a paper cone and made of crushed ice drenched in syrup---lemon, lime, strawberry, grape, spearmint or cherry--- the snowball was a potent aid to cooling off. There were snowball stands all over town, but none of them seemed to top the sweet confections of our own itinerant vendor.

In the evening after dinner the whole family gathered on the porch. We rocked and talked as twilight deepened into darkness and the soothing sounds of night began. As the vibrant humming of the locusts waxed and waned, the rhythmic creaking of our rocking chairs mingled with the footsteps of passersby. The mournful hooting of boats and ships came from the direction of the river, and sometimes we could even hear the roaring of the lions at the Audubon Park Zoo. Now and then the barking of a dog or a rousing cat fight would disturb the peace and occasionally we heard the crowing of a rooster mistaken in his timing.

On those nights the porch was a serene and pleasant haven where the different generations not only communicated but actually enjoyed being together. As long as we children managed to be reasonably well-behaved, we were encouraged to contribute our share to the conversation. On the other hand, we enjoyed listening when the adults became involved in a subject that interested us.

My grandfather held us spellbound with stories of his youth. "Tell us about the olden days," we would ask him, and he would graciously comply. He was a marvellous raconteur, and I believe he enjoyed reminiscing as much as we enjoyed listening. When our handsome young uncles spent an evening on the porch it was a real treat, for we considered them the epitome of sophistication and *savior faire*. They loved to talk, arguing endlessly but amicably about sports events and the news of the day.

My father, always eager to instill in us his interest in science, would sometimes take advantage of a clear night to give us a lesson in astronomy. From the yard he would point out the Milky Way, the constellations and each visible planet. Then, back on the porch, he wove a fascinating tapestry of galaxies and supernovae, comets, and satellites, light years and phases of the moon. Our minds were fired with wonder and curiosity, and we bombarded Daddy with questions. Two questions that always led to a lively discussion were: "Is there life on other planets?" and "Will we ever reach the moon?" This last question has now, of course, been answered. How I wish my father had been here to see the answer unfolding in the first breathtaking landing on the moon. And how completely I was able to identify with it because of those evenings on the porch long ago.

My Mother's love of nature's beauty was the perfect complement to Daddy's fascination with its mystery. During our evenings on the porch she called our attention to moonlight and shadows, the sounds of the night, the caress of a breeze, and the perfume of flowers in the garden. Nothing lovely escaped her. My whole childhood, in fact, was permeated with the *leit-motif* of Mother's voice, calling "Come outside and see!" She presented us with rainstorms and rainbows, blazing sunsets and the glories of the night sky. Sometimes her gift was a passing cloud formation, a newly opened rose, or a butterfly glittering in the sunshine. Although she took great delight in these things because of their beauty, she also saw in them a proof of God's presence and a reflection of His glory. Consequently, we children were instilled with a sense of the sacred along with the aesthetic and learned to equate beauty and joy with God.

One of the chief assets of the porch was plenty of fresh air. Mother always said that fresh air was good for us, especially for our appetites. How right she was. When I remember the amount of food we consumed during our summers on the porch, my calorie-counting brain reels. We seemed, in fact, be be on a perpetual picnic, keeping up our strength between meals with grapes and bananas washed down with milk or lemonade.

It was always a treat to have our friends over for an alfresco lunch. Since Brother and his cronies made it a practice to eat on the run, up and down the front steps and in an out of the yard, Rosie accommodated them with a movable feast of sandwiches, pickles, and potato chips served directly from the kitchen. But for me and my friends, it was a different story. Mother felt that it was one thing for boys to eat like Tarzan of the Apes or, as Rosie said, a gang of gorillas, but girls should try, at least, to act like little ladies. So shimmering aspics, chicken *à la* king and dainty finger sandwiches were par for the course for us. These goodies were served on a card table set *de rigueur* with gleaming china, crystal and silver on a snowy embroidered tea cloth. This midsummer elegance unfailingly transformed us into the little ladies that Mother expected us to be, at least for the duration of the meal. Although the male contingent hooted rudely at our luncheon arrangements, they quickly changed their tune when dessert time rolled around. This *piece de résistance*, served alike to both camps, was usually a gorgeous sundae or banana split, dripping with whipped cream, cherries and nuts. I can see now that this was really living, and even at the time, I must admit, I rather suspected that it was.

Despite the fact that Rosie was the source of all our feasting, she often predicted a stomachache in our immediate future. "Mark my words," she'd tell us, "You chillun will be sick mighty soon if you don't stop pushin' food into your mouths." But the prospect of illness left us unconcerned for we had a physician of our very own at home. One of our handsome young uncles was a doctor and, though busy night and day, was always there when needed. We didn't care for the awful tasting medicine he often prescribed but he always made us smile or, for that matter, laugh and---better still---he cured us.

Although some porches, and always the sleeping porch, were screened, our front porch was wide open to the elements. One of those elements was the mosquito. Sometimes only one or two mosquitoes buzzed around but, occasionally, especially on summer nights, hoards of them attacked us. When that happened, Daddy wielded the Flit gun, spraying furiously until the buzzing pests were vanquished. If replacements flew in, their numbers were usually small enough for us to handle with the swat of a hand or of a fan. This defensive action was, of course, a secondary function of our fans, their primary function being to create a breeze. Daddy, Grandpa and my uncles used stiff palmetto fans, Mother and I used dainty folding fans but Brother, spurning all fans, stirred up a breeze by means of perpetual motion. While we rocked and fanned, he tore around the yard in pursuit of lightning bugs. These shining creatures, also known as fireflies, had, at least for me, a mysterious beauty akin to that of falling stars, and it made me sad when Brother caught them. One by one, he put them in a glass jar whose top was punched with holes, gradually filling the jar until it glimmered like a lantern. But Mother, to my relief and Brother's gloom, always insisted that he release his captives before going inside for the night.

Rainy days always brought a welcome respite from the heat and sometimes, to the delight of the juvenile population, the excitement of a flood. Since the water seldom rose higher than the bottom step, these floods could be classed as an inconvenience rather than a catastrophe. Lawns and flower beds became temporary swamps, and irate motorists in stalled cars dotted the flooded streets. Anyone who kept a skiff or pirogue in the garage would launch it for a cruise around the neighborhood. Even the irate motorists were erstwhile yachtsmen who had driven at top speed to make bow waves in the water. Waders and splashers popped up everywhere. Some of the boys, my future husband among them, brought little sailboats made of pieces of wood with paper sails. They raced them near the drains where the water made swift eddies as it began to recede. The gay holiday atmosphere continued at full tilt until the water finally drained away, and the whole aquatic scene disappeared as completely as if it had been a mirage.

The safe, secure, yet fascinating relationship of porch and street was one of the most pleasant aspects of my youth. When out of doors there was always something to see, something to do and someone to do it with. Although there was little, if any, adult visiting between the porches on our block, friendly waves and smiles were neighborly expressions of good will. The steady stream of pedestrians that passed our house was not only a diversion but also a protective screen. Even at night there were many people walking by---some of them for pleasure or for exercise and others on their way to the drugstore or the movies. Mother and Daddy were often in their number, for they loved to walk at night and also to go to the show. There was a very real, though unofficial teamwork to our outdoor ambiance, for just as the walkers protected us, we on the porches protected them. Indeed, together we kept the streets and neighborhoods of the city safe.

Although summer was the *raison d'être* of the porch, the semi-tropical climate of New Orleans made it a place for all seasons. Autumn with its crisp and invigorating nip was a perfect time to be on the porch. So was springtime when Nature was at its peak. And since balmy, springlike Christmas days are a New Orleans specialty, the front porch, wearing a big wreath with a fat red bow, was an integral part of our holiday festivities.

One after another the seasons passed and with them the years of childhood. Windows were gradually dotted with air-conditioning units, and the television set became a household fixture. These modern Pied Pipers lured us inside and held us captive, mesmerizing us with cool comfort and passive pleasure while they rang down the curtain on the saga of the porch.

Winter by the Fire

Another piper lured us inside in the winter. This piper was the fire that burned in all our grates. Only a small percentage of the city's houses were centrally heated and ours was not among them. Open fires were, therefore, very much a part of our winter way of life.

Our vintage Victorian house was crowned with chimneys and adorned with a fireplace in every room. On cold days fires were lighted to give the gas radiators a booster shot of heat, but on cool days they were lighted simply for the pleasure they afforded us. My mother was a firm believer in beauty for its own sake and loved to have the house suffused with firelight. This meant that all the chimneys must be swept and scoured before the first cool spell arrived.

At the end of summer, chimney sweeps in top hats and tails descended on the city like a flock of giant blackbirds. They announced their presence with a strident, wailing chant. "Ramonez," they cried, "Ramonez vos chiminés." Meaning, "Sweep out your chimneys."

My mother, anxious to get a head start on winter, was always glad to see them, but my brother and I greeted them with a blend of fear and fascination. The charcoal and soot that was smeared on their black faces gave them an eerie, ashen appearance, and the pack of tools on their backs made them seem deformed. Indeed, they looked like hunchbacks beneath their load of brooms, brushes, weights, coils of rope and bundles of twigs.

Yet their cry held a promise of excitement that sucked us outside like needles to a magnet. We couldn't help but notice that despite their heavy load there was an air of cockiness about them. Some of them emphasized this by wearing the top hats that were their badge of trade at a rakish angle and by walking with as much of a swagger as their backpacks would allow. They seemed to be proclaiming that their job was not an ordinary one but work that called for skill and virtuosity. And so it did. Once on the roof-tops the sweeps were not only masters of their trade but daring aerialists as fearless and surefooted as the airborne creatures they resembled.

While the chimney sweeps were still at work, coal vendors driving creak-ing, mule-drawn wagons made their rounds. Frequent stops and starts along the way marked their progress as they hawked their gleaming, blue-black merchandise. Our coal, however, was delivered via dump truck, much to my chagrin and Brother's. But regardless of its manner of delivery the coal soon rose in glittering mini-mountains in backyards all over town.

At last the time was ripe for a whirlwind that tore into the city and swept it clean each fall. This explosion of dusting, sweeping, polishing and embel-lishing was known as fall housecleaning. At our house my mother, the maid, the cook, the washwoman and even the gardener fell upon their work with the ardor of zealots and ripped the house apart from stem to stern. Within a week they transformed it from a cool and casual, rushmatted, slipcovered, porch-oriented summer house into a handsome, snug and inward looking winter household of shimmering velvets, deep piled Oriental rugs and polished grates laid with coal and kindling.

Now that the house was ready for winter, we waited impatiently for the first cool snap to come. A chilly morning finally dawned and with it the glorious surprise of a room aglow with firelight. For once there was no prob-lem about getting up. A fire danced before my eager eyes, and with a hop, skip and jump I was toasting myself on the hearth rug. Once dressed I rushed through the unheated regions of the upstairs hall, joining forces there with Brother, down the stairs, through the entrance hall and into the dining room where another fire was blazing. Breakfast, usually regarded with disdain, was now devoured with pleasure. Even oatmeal tasted good!

The fireside that was our childhood favorite was the one in the big old-fashioned kitchen. It wasn't an ordinary fireplace, but an enormous black iron stove that stood before the brick chimney wall. This coal eating, fire breathing colossus was the pride and joy of Rosie, our cook. I can see her now as she manipulated it, lifting the lids to check the fire, opening the drafts to inspect the oven heat, stirring the coals until the sparks flew and cooking everything from soup to mouth-watering desserts. A gas range stood white and pristine against the opposite wall, but Rosie regarded it with suspicion and contempt, refusing to touch it until the dog days of summer forced her hand.

Rosie was a true virtuoso of the pots and pans and coaxed culinary symphonies from her archaic range. All day long a soup pot simmered on a back burner. One sniff was enough to inform us of its contents. The standby soup was vegetable, but Rosie's specialities were crawfish bisque and gumbo, seafood gumbo year round and turkey gumbo after Christmas and Thanksgiving.

She had a way with seafood that turned meatless Fridays into feast days. Jambalaya, redfish courtboullion, shrimp Creole, and crawfish étoufée were all dishes that we feasted on routinely. She also had a way with pastry. Her quick, light touch turned out biscuits, pies and shortcakes that were irresistably crisp and delicate. But, unbelievably, it was grits that Brother and I liked best of all. Red beans and rice and fried trout were perennial runners-up, but grits remained our all time favorite. Anything that Rosie served with grits was sure to be a favorite; grillades and grits, kidney stew and grits, golden squares of fried grits and even liver and grits meant mealtime bliss to us.

Holidays were Rosie's forte. She baked a gaily decorated ham for Easter, whipped up doughnuts for Mardi Gras and cooked a batch of blackeyed peas for luck on New Year's Eve. But it wasn't until Christmas that she pulled out all the stops to create a soaring crescendo of cooking that culminated in the glories of our Christmas dinner and the open house that followed.

During the weeks leading up to Christmas, her radiant range was the hub of the household for Brother and me. Even the promise of Santa Claus paled before it. Drawn by the heady aromas that emanated from its bright red depths, we were constantly under Rosie's feet. She made a valiant attempt to keep us occupied, giving us nuts to crack, dates to stuff, and popcorn and cranberries to string for the tree. We also stacked pralines in paper-lined tins and filled glass jars with shelled pecans.

However, we never lost sight of the main attraction. As far as we were concerned, the stove was a stage and Rosie a magician who worked wonders on it. We sniffed ecstatically at the scent of baking cakes and pies and waited impatiently for cookies and gingerbread men to pop out of the oven. Our appetites increased each day as Rosie measured and poured, kneaded and stirred. As time went on she was hard put to keep us satisfied without seriously depleting her stores. I'd like to think she missed us when we deserted her on Christmas Eve, Santa Claus upstaging her at last, but if she did I'm sure it was with mixed emotions.

The kitchen was a private domain that Brother and I shared with Rosie. It was strictly off limits to the adults of the family. Gathering around the fire as a family unit was either in the dining room during meals or in the sitting room after dinner. On winter evenings the sitting room was a cozy, fire-lit retreat. Its walls were lined with bookcases, and it was furnished with comfortable armchairs that were somewhat battered from constant use. Its most outstanding furnishings were a big combination radio-phonograph and an antique mahogany cabinet that held Daddy's collection of records. If the radio wasn't turned on, the phonograph was playing, and our evenings were filled with music, laughter, every timbre of the human voice, periodic intrusions of static, and, always in the background, the cheerful hiss and crackle of the fire.

We were a family with a well-developed sense of humor, and the radio programs we liked best were the comedy shows. In those days the radio was a happy hunting ground for comedians. The sound waves rocked with their wit and jocularity, and so did we. The high jinks of Jack Benny, Fred Allen, Henry Morgan, George Burns and Gracie Allen kept us in stiches. So did the antics of Ed Wynn, Edgar Bergen, Jimmy Durante, Amos and Andy and Fibber Magee and Molly.

Although we preferred the comedians, there was a wide variety of shows to choose from. My favorites were *The Lux Radio Theatre* which was announced by Cecil B. de Mille, *Major Bowes' Amateur Hour*, whose gong was the voice of doom to the contestants, *Your Hit Parade*, a medley of current popular tunes and *Lights Out*, a horror show that was announced by a creepy, quivering voice that made my blood run cold. But as much as I liked it, I seldom listened to *Lights Out*, for it whipped up my imagination to such a point that I was paralyzed by fear and plagued by sleepless nights. Brother, however, thought *Lights Out* was funny and amused himself by creeping up behind me with realistic imitations of its sound effects. Brother was also a fan of *The Lone Ranger*, a western noted for its galloping hoofbeats and the Ranger's strident cry of "Hi-Yo Silver," and of *Gangbusters*, a show that I abhorred.

The radio brought many of the major events and personalities of the day into our sitting room. There were, for instance, the fireside chats of President Roosevelt, the abdication speech of Edward VIII and the extended news coverage after the assassination of Huey P. Long. But it wasn't until the broadcast of Orson Wells' Mercury Theatre production of H. G. Wells' *War of the*

Worlds in 1938 that the great impact of radio was fully realized. Many of those who heard the program panicked, convinced that we were in the throes of an invasion from Mars. Men armed themselves---a number of them volunteering for the National Guard---mothers gathered their families around them, cars full of people fleeing the supposed invaders jammed the highways, and many who stayed behind prayed together in the streets. To this day, I regret missing this amazing program and wonder what my reaction to it would have been.

When we played the phonograph it was classical music all the way, especially the compositions of Bach, Beethoven, Brahms and Wagner. Daddy was the musical mentor of the family, and these composers were his favorites. Such glorious music surely doesn't need embellishment, yet I always felt it took on added luster when the room was filled with firelight. Wagner's operas, especially, seemed to rise and fall and go in tandem with the flickering flames. Daddy wasn't an opera buff, preferring symphonies and chamber music, but he loved the operas of Wagner. Even now their soaring melodies conjure up for me a picture of our sitting room, the glow of firelight and my father listening intently to his beloved music.

Our living room, or parlor, as we called it, was a formal room reserved for special occasions such as holidays and parties. Christmas Eve was one of those occasions. It was then that Sants Claus came to our house instead of on Christmas morning. Not satisfied with arriving at this unusual hour, he also came in an unorthodox way. Although there was a wealth of chimneys on our roof, he came on foot to our front door. Furthermore it was the sound of a little silver bell, remarkably like the one that Rosie rang to summon us to meals, and not the sound of sleighbells that alerted us to his arrival. However, Brother and I were bursting with such excitement that Santa's arrangements didn't phase us. He could have come on roller skates for all we cared.

Everyone was laughing and talking when we greeted him at the front door. Then as he stepped over the threshhold, a hush fell upon us. The moment we were waiting for had come. As Brother and I watched wide-eyed, the great sliding doors of the parlor were thrown open to reveal a glowing, firelit room filled to the brim with Christmas. For one split second before we rushed in to receive our gifts, we stood rooted to the spot spellbound by the huge glittering tree, the lovely little creche beneath it, the gaily colored toys we had so longed for and stacks of tempting and mysterious packages.

During the Twelve Days of Christmas the parlor continued to radiate the good cheer of the season. Firelight and tree light shone on an endless stream of callers. There was such a giving and receiving of gifts that the floor was periodically flooded with ribbons and tissue paper, and the walls reverberated with juvenile squeals and adult murmurs of delight.

The refreshments mother served were Rosie's melt-in-the-mouth confections. A marble-topped table was drawn before the fire and laden with her Christmas sweets. Pralines and crystallized fruits were heaped in cut-glass compotes, and cocoons, macaroons, meringue kisses, and Bourbon balls arranged on silver trays. A decorated fruitcake rested grandly on a crystal cake-stand and petit fours iced in Yuletide red and green nestled in a silver basket. Every conceivable kind of cookie was represented, including the lace cookies that Brother and I liked best of all. Although these cookies were made with the oatmeal we so cordially detested, they were delicate and wafer thin. If we hadn't actually seen them in the making we would have found it impossible to believe that they contained the formidable *bête noir* of our breakfasts.

A pair of sparkling cut-glass decanters stood at one end of the table. They were filled with amber-colored sherry that gleamed like liquid gold in the reflection of the fire. The sherry was for the grownups but there was eggnog for us. It was served directly from the kitchen and was sadly lacking, although we didn't know it, the ingredient that Mother called "the real thing." We of course, didn't need "the real thing," being super-animated without it. In fact, with each passing day Brother and I became increasingly keyed up until finally, to the relief of everyone, the perpetual party came to a halt on Twelfth Night. The next day the tree was taken down, the creche stored away, the fire extinguished, and the big sliding doors closed.

When Brother and I were very young, we shared a bedroom with each other and also with Mary, our nurse. On winter nights a fire always burned in the grate. Far from the buoyant blaze that woke us in the morning, it was a subdued fire of small, winking flames that whispered to us as they died down for the night. When Mary turned out the lamp we were suddenly submerged in a shimmering light that was as rosy as a sunset. Shifting shadows played fitfully all around us, and we soon became one with them by making shadows of our very own. As long as we could stay awake, our busy little hands and fingers created animated silhouettes that frisked and pranced at our command up and down and all around the pink washed walls and ceiling.

Later on when we were older and I had a bedroom and a fireplace to myself, the childhood habit of making shadow images prevailed. But this time they were made in my imagination. Night after night, as the dying embers flared and fell, I lay wide-eyed in my bed and made up story after story. The heroine of these tales was always me. I was forever beautiful, charming, wise and pursued by handsome suitors, a far cry from my real adolescent self. Courtship and weddings were the nucleus of my fiction. The very soul of fickleness, I walked down the aisle innumerable times toward dozens of different grooms. My wedding dress grew in splendor, my veil in length and my engagement ring in size with each of these processions.

Another favorite role was that of most popular girl at the prom. Cast in this part, I was steeped in self-confidence, corsaged in gardenias, and "broken" by the stag line every ten or fifteen seconds.

Sometimes I was a movie star, usually with Robert Taylor in hot pursuit. In this guise I affected a cigarette holder between clenched teeth and, dripping orchids and white fox furs, dispensed autographs to my adoring fans.

In those days the national pastime of outdoor cooking was still an event of the future; yet each Monday morning a charcoal brazier burned in our backyard. Seated on top of it was a tubful of wash that boiled and bubbled furiously. This steaming cauldron was tended by Lucy, our straw-hatted, pipe-smoking washwoman. Between bouts with the washboard and the clothesline she poured bluing into the water and stirred the laundry with a long, soggy wooden pole. If she could have looked into a crystal ball to see the evolution of her humble brazier, she would have been astonished. For now it is called a hibachi and cooks steaks and shishkabobs instead of the family wash.

It was delightful to grow up in the glow of firelight. Our many firesides filled the house with symbolic as well as actual warmth and bound us all together in a very special way. Indeed, to me, they were a living presence that evoked a sense of mystery, wonder and tranquility no central heating system has since been able to inspire.

Canal Street - The Dividing Line

One of my first recollections of leaving my neighborhood was to go shopping with my mother on Canal Street. When she said "I have to go to 'town' and I'd like you to come with me" I knew that meant taking a bath, getting all dressed up and catching the bus to Canal Street for a day's trekking around to all the department stores up and down on both sides of that broad expanse.

Canal Street was the hub of the city's main shopping and commercial center. It was the dividing line between uptown and downtown. It was the orientation point of streets and most of the public transporation routes throughout the city. Canal Street was like a magnet drawing New Orleanians "up" from downtown, "down" from uptown and "in" from the suburbs.

My main impression of Canal Street when I was little was that it was big, and busy, and noisy. Those early shopping trips were a real drag. I woefully trailed after my mother as she systematically made her way through all her favorite stores, D. H. Holmes, Maison Blanche, Godchaux's, Gus Mayer, Marks Isaacs and Mayer Israel (the last two stores no longer exist) and all the way down to Krauss at the corner of Canal and Basin Street, a five-block walk from D. H. Holmes.

When she saw that my flagging spirits needed reviving, she ducked into the Kress Five and Ten Cent Store (on Canal between Dauphine and Burgundy) where the first sight to greet my eyes was the enormous candy counter lining the left-hand wall as you walked in. There, in bin after bin, was enough candy to sink the Good Ship Lollipop, in every color, size, shape and flavor imaginable. I would walk up and down the aisle, examining each bin, my energies entirely restored. There were licorice sticks, candy corn, lemon drops and orange drops, chocolate-covered peanuts and raisins, peppermints, bittersweets, candy hearts, jawbreakers, silver bells, toffee, banana slices, malted milk balls, wax candies and many others. Best of all, you could mix them all up. I took almost as much time to make my selections as my mother took to make hers in the fabric department at Krauss. I usually wound up with five cents of candy corn, five cents of lemon drops, and five cents of chocolate covered raisins. (Our dentist was conveniently located in the Audubon Building next door to Kress).

Once in a while Mother and I would enjoy a triple-decker sandwich at the Kress luncheon counter, munching away to the lively strains of popular medlies played by organist Ray McNamara, perched on a balcony at the back of the store.

At that age I had no appreciation for the phenomenal majesty of Canal Street (didn't every city have a main street like ours?) or its curious and colorful history. Since then I've read John Chase's delightful book *Frenchmen, Desire, Good Children* about New Orleans streets and have learned about Canal Street's unusual origins. It became one of the widest streets in the country through a fluke in city planning and was named Canal Street for a canal that was never dug. When French settlers built their fortified town on the banks of the Mississippi, the area that's now Canal Street was outside the town boundaries. It became an overgrown and unused "commons" (unclaimed property for common use). After the Louisiana Purchase New Orleans claimed it as city property and the federal government recognized the claim with the stipulation that a 50-foot wide navigable canal be dug down the middle of the expanse from the Mississippi River to the Carondelet Canal at Basin Street. Sixty-foot borders were reserved on both sides of the proposed waterway. Not a spadeful of dirt was ever turned for the purpose of creating a canal on Canal Street, so the city inadvertently became blessed with a main thoroughfare that measures one hundred and seventy-one feet across. (The extra foot may be an appropriate bit of lagniappe.)

Canal Street had the distinction of being a beneficiary in the will of prominent New Orleans merchant and philanthropist Judah Touro. When he died in 1854 he left between $200,000 and $300,000 for the beautification of the street that he had helped to establish as the city's major commercial thoroughfare.

The part of Canal Street history that most intrigued me was its role as the dividing line between the Creoles and the Americans. When Americans began pouring into the city after the Louisiana Purchase and it became apparent that the French-speaking Creoles were not going to make room for them in the Vieux Carré (or in their social and cultural life either), the Americans developed their own settlement on the other side of Canal Street, which was the beginning of uptown. The broad expanse that separated the two antagonistic groups was known as "neutral ground," a kind of "no man's land." Ever since then we've called the median separating all the city's wide streets the "neutral ground." Antagonism between the Creole section and the American section of the city was so intense that in 1836 the state created a separate municipality for each section (and a third for the rest of the city), a political situation that continued for sixteen years until the sections were reunited under a single governing body.

The Americans built residences and businesses up and down Canal Street until it gradually developed into the bustling commercial and entertainment center that I first became acquainted with as a child.

In spite of the exhausting shopping trips with my mother, I found Canal Street exciting. It was where we spent Mardi Gras day, along with thousands of other New Orleanians, prancing up and down the street and shouting "Throw me something, Mister" as the Rex parade went lumbering by. It was where we went during the Christmas holidays to walk in wonder through the lobby of the Roosevelt Hotel (now the Fairmont), completely decked out in angel hair like a white cotton candy cocoon; and then to stroll past the windows of Holmes and Maison Blanche, filled with ingenious displays of animated elves, dolls, soldiers, fairies and other delightful Christmas-time creatures. It was where we went to buy our Easter outfits and our first high-heeled shoes.

Canal Street was a shopping area primarily for the white citizens of New Orleans. Although we saw an occasional Negro in the department stores---which had separate drinking fountains for white and colored---Negroes had their own shopping area on South Rampart Street right off Canal and on Dryades Street and Felicity Street.

When my friends and I were allowed to go to Canal Street by ourselves for the first time, at about age twelve, we knew we had reached a milestone in our growing-up years. Now when we went to Canal Street it meant "going out"---dressing up, doing something special. As we grew older we wouldn't have dreamed of going to "town" without high-heeled shoes, hats, and gloves. As teenagers, my friends and I considered a Saturday on Canal Street a special treat. We'd meet under the clock at D. H. Holmes, have lunch in the Holmes dining room, spend part of the afternoon window-shopping and wind up a perfect day at one of the big movie houses.

The strip of Canal Street that we called "town" stretched from the river to Claiborne Avenue. Beyond Claiborne, Canal continued straight as an arrow all the way to the cemeteries at City Park Avenue. This was a largely residential thoroughfare and bore little resemblance to the busy center closer to the river.

There was was one building on Canal Street's bustling shopping strip, however, that looked like a residence and stood out among the retail stores surrounding it. That was the exclusive Boston Club at 824 Canal, next door to Godchaux's Clothing Store. We sometimes saw a meticulously uniformed black man polishing the brass on the front door as we walked past the Club, heading from Godchaux's to Mayer Israel in the next block. This sedate scene contrasted sharply with the pandemonium of Mardi Gras day when the Queen of Carnival and her maids were ensconced on a special balcony across the facade of the Club. Here it was that Rex, Ruler of Carnival, stopped to salute and toast his Queen as thousands of paradegoers watched and cheered. The building was originally constructed as a residence in 1857 and became the home of the Boston Club in 1887. It always appeared impeccably manicured, seemingly in wait for the next Carnival visitation. Believed to be the second oldest private men's club in the United States, the socially elite Boston Club was not named after a city, as I long believed, but after a card game.

Sometimes on a Saturday expedition to "town," if we had a few minutes to kill before our movie started, we visited the Jesuit Church on Baronne Street right around the corner from the Boston Club. Officially named the Church of the Immaculate Conception, everyone called it the Jesuit Church after the religious order that staffs it. We thought it very grand compared to our parish church of St. Rose de Lima. It had a majestic air of solemnity and dignity despite the throngs of people passing in and out of its massive wooden doors and the long lines of penitents crowding the aisles waiting to go to confession. Our visits were not so much pious as curious. As we quietly knelt in one of the lacy cast iron pews we were not praying; we were sightseeing. This was an exotic looking church! The domes, columns and arches marked with delicate tracery reminded us of a scene from the Arabian Nights. The gilt bronze altar was so dazzling we thought it was gold. The stained glass windows, the elaborate silver candelabra, the columned galleries high in the nave all in turn captured our rapt attention. As our gaze finally centered on the white marble statue of the Blessed Mother with her halo of electric lights in a lofty niche above the altar, we were reminded of where we were.

We said a quick "Hail Mary" and scrupulously blessed ourselves with holy water as we passed the huge marble fonts on the way out.

Just around the next block from the Jesuit Church was the Hibernia Bank Building, its 23 stories topped by a round white cupola. The Hibernia's observation tower was the highest point in the city at that time. The cupola was particularly pretty at night when it was all lighted, looking like a miniature Greek temple. Once my father took Benny and me up to the tower, and for the first time I got a panoramic view of the city. We could see the bend in the river and all the way out to Lake Pontchartrain. My father pointed out the New Basin Canal and Huey Long Bridge. We even thought we could see City Park and our own neighborhood.

Canal Street was the transportation hub of New Orleans and the point of orientation for traveling around the city. Besides dividing uptown from downtown, it also divided north from south. All the streets on the uptown side of Canal Street are designated South and those on the downtown side are designated North. Sometimes we found ourselves on Canal Street even when we weren't heading there on purpose for business or pleasure. Almost all the streetcar and bus lines began and ended their routes on Canal Street and if we had to transfer from one line to another, we often did it on Canal. The neutral ground was almost like a train station, with four lanes of streetcars screeching and clanging up and down all day and most of the night.

There was a real train station on Canal Street at Basin Street, between Krauss Department Store and the Saenger Theater---the Southern Railway Station. We sometimes wandered through its ornate entrance to watch the trains and their passengers, getting a vicarious taste of travel and far-away places. The Southern station was demolished when the new Union Passenger Terminal opened in 1954.

Most of my travel was by bus, often the Esplanade bus on the way to Canal Street---an adventure in itself. From the time I got on the bus at North Broad and Esplanade until I alighted at Canal and Dauphine Street I was enthralled with the view out of the bus window. As many times as I traveled the route, I never tired of inspecting the old mansions along Esplanade Avenue, some of them converted into rooming houses with multiple mail boxes lining their entrances, or into nursing homes with cane rockers inhabiting their front porches. Despite these indignities to their aristocratic origins, they still presented a facade of melancholy grandeur to the passerby. Once in a while a beautiful old home with Corinthian columns and leaded-glass doors came in view, its garden meticulously groomed and ironwork fence freshly painted, standing in shining contrast to its down-at-the-heels neighbors. At Esplanade and North Rampart the mood of the historic avenue was sharply broken by the noisy activity of St. Aloysius High School, its yard often filled with boys playing ball. On the other side of North Rampart I always glanced to the right to catch a glimpse of the Italian Union Hall, the elegant building which was the cultural meeting place of the city's Italian community. I didn't know it at the time but the building was originally one of the grand residences of New Orleans. Built in 1835 for William Nott, first Dutch consular representative in the city, it became the property of prominent New Orleans lawyer and United States Senator John Slidell, who presented it as a wedding present to his sister-in-law and her husband, General P. G. T. Beauregard. The elaborate Italian facade I so much admired from the bus window conceals the original Greek Revival front designed by James Gallier, Sr.

This part of Esplanade on down to the river was known as the Promenade Publique during the days when the city's Creole aristocracy lived in mansions lining each side of the neutral ground. The Creoles enjoyed Sunday afternoon strolls under the magnolias, elms, and oaks shading the Avenue. Their presence seemed to linger still along the tree-shrouded street, for the mood subtly shifted as my bus passed North Rampart and headed for the city's core, the Vieux Carré.

The French Quarter

At Dauphine and Esplanade my bus turned right. We were in the Vieux Carré. Without being told, I knew we must be in the oldest part of town. Vieux Carré is French for Old Quarter, but I never called it the Vieux Carré, just the French Quarter, a name that derived naturally from the original French-speaking inhabitants of the section. Because of the preponderance of Italian vendors and merchants in the area when I was growing up, you heard more Italian being spoken than French. My father used to say it should be called the "Italian Quarter."

Whatever we called it, it was the site of the original French settlement, planned as a typical French fortified town with streets laid out in a neat grid pattern. That pattern is much the same today as it was when French engineer Adrien de Pauger supervised the building of the city. In fact, the Quarter has one of the oldest street plans still in use in the country. The Quarter's boundaries, slightly expanded from that original grid, run from Canal Street to upper Esplanade and from North Rampart to the Mississippi River.

As my bus followed its tortuous route up Dauphine Street, lurching and bumping along through the Quarter, I took in the scene from my window. The narrow roadway seemed to close in on the bus after the broad expanse of Esplanade Avenue. Houses were huddled close together, separated from the street by a narrow banquette. Most of them were old green-shuttered cottages or step-on-the-banquette doubles, some with dormer windows or garrets. Many looked dilapidated, including the cottage at 505 Dauphine where John James Audubon once lived and worked on his famous *Birds of America*. Occasionally I caught a glimpse of a courtyard dominated by banana trees and palms. There were not many grand houses on Dauphine. Most of

the show places of the Quarter were over on Bourbon Street and Royal Street and in the area around Jackson Square. As I remember it, the Quarter had a general air of dilapidation or decay about it, mingled with an aura of mystery, romance, and adventure.

Although I knew little about the history of the city at the time, I sensed the "old" quality of the Quarter and its "foreign" ambience. Other neighborhoods were different from my own, but the Quarter was the most different. It wasn't just the buildings with their ironwork balconies and green courtyards bunched so close together along the narrow streets; or the cobblestone alleyways; or the antique and souvenir shops, or even the imposing architectural setting around Jackson Square. It was, perhaps, first of all, the aromas. As soon as you entered the Quarter your nose told you where you were. Nowhere else in the city were you assailed with such a variety and intensity of odors: coffee wafting from the Morning Call, olive oil and salted cod from the Central Grocery, strawberries from the farmer's market, seafood from the French Market stalls, malt from the Jax Brewery, and sometimes the scent of sweet olive from Jackson Square, contrasting sharply with the dusty smell of the Cabildo across the street.

In spite of the Cabildo's dusty smell, I loved going there. Once in a while on a Sunday morning my father would gather up Benny, Helen, and me and take us to visit the museums at the Cabildo and the Presbytère. I was always more interested in the things on display inside these impressive buildings than I was in the buildings themselves or their important place in the city's history. The Cabildo had been the seat of government for the colony under Spanish rule, and the Presbytère, although intended as a rectory, was actually used first for stores and apartments, and later as a courthouse. Between the two buildings, separated by Pirate's Alley and St. Anthony's Alley, rose the St. Louis Cathedral. All three buildings face Jackson Square and the river. This is the very heart of the city, the core around which the rest of the city was planned.

Jackson Square, originally called the Place d'Armes, was the parade ground for French and later Spanish militia in colonial days. It was re-named in 1851 in honor of General Andrew Jackson, the hero of the Battle of New Orleans.

As we headed for the Cabildo, my mind was usually on another figure in New Orleans history, Jean Laffite. The pirate was one of my favorite local heroes and even to this day I think of Jean Laffite the minute I set foot in the Cabildo. I never tired of hearing my father tell us the tale of how Governor Claiborne put a price on Laffite's head and wanted to clap him in prison; and how the pirate helped General Jackson win the Battle of New Orleans. We viewed the prison cells in the Cabildo with childish awe, duly impressed with the display featuring Laffite's tools of trade: spy glass, powder horn, compass, ship's lantern, folding knives and water jug, all claimed to be from his pirate ship. (Jean Laffite was never imprisoned in the Cabildo, but his brother Pierre was.) The ultimate fate of Lafitte, still shrouded in mystery, further piqued our interest and curiosity. I always pictured him sailing off into the sunset, lost forever in clouds of romance and further adventure.

When we had our fill of Laffite we headed for the second floor of the Cabildo where we transferred our attention to the death mask of Napoleon. As I recall, the mask reposed majestically on a red velvet cloth inside a large glass case in the center of the room known as the Sala Capitular, or Transfer Room. This was the room where the transfer of Louisiana from France to the United States took place in 1803. We were always strangely fascinated by this macabre exhibit. On one of our French Quarter jaunts my father walked us by the Napoleon House at 500 Chartres Street, just a couple of blocks away from the Cabildo. "This is where Napoleon was going to live if he had ever come to New Orleans," he told us, pointing to the three-story building. It seems that the Creoles in New Orleans were crazy about Napoleon. After he was exiled to St. Helena, a particularly enthusiastic group of Creole gentlemen concocted a plot to rescue him from the island and bring him to New Orleans. The mayor of the city, Nicholas Girod, graciously offered his home as the Emperor's proposed dwelling place. Napoleon's untimely death dashed their daredevil plans, but Mayor Girod's house came to be known as the Napoleon House thereafter. Thirteen years after Napoleon died in 1821, his personal physician Dr. Francisco Antommarchi moved to New Orleans and actually had an office in this same building. It was he who made the city a gift of the Emperor's death mask, cast from a mold Dr. Antommarchi made forty hours after Napoleon died.

The death mask has had an exotic history. It was moved from the Cabildo to the "new" City Hall (Gallier Hall) in 1853 where it was exhibited in the Council Chamber. Right after the Civil War it was thrown out and retrieved from a trash pile by the city treasurer who kept it as his personal property. It passed into other hands, winding up in Atlanta, but was finally returned to the city in 1909 and was again installed in the Cabildo. It can be viewed there today, along with many other items of Napoleonic memorabilia.

There were other exhibits at the Cabildo---Carnival costumes, ships' models, furniture, old manuscripts, papers and portraits, but none so captured our attention or were so memorable as the Laffite and Napoleon exhibits.

From the Cabildo we went to the Presbytère, which at that time had displays of Louisiana flora and fauna and a great collection of fish and game. From its name, meaning "priest's house" in French, we assumed that the Presbytère had been the rectory for the priests of the St. Louis Cathedral. Not so. Although the first two buildings on this site had served that purpose, the present Presbytère building had originally housed shops and apartments and later provided space for several courts. It became a part of the Louisiana State Museum in 1911. One wing of the Presbytère was devoted to exhibitions of Louisiana wildlife in their natural settings. The animals looked so life-like to me it seemed as though they could have stepped right through their glass display cases. A big black bear with shiny eyes and long, sharp claws gave me a fright no matter how many times I saw him, frozen as he was in time and space, forever poised to pounce on an unsuspecting muskrat. I don't know which we liked best, the animals or the fish. We were familiar with lots of the fish on display because of summer trips to the Gulf Coast where my father and Benny caught fish just like many of the ones on exhibit---speckled trout, sheepshead, redfish, stingrays, flounder, catfish, and spade fish. Not far from the fish collection were the snakes. After a quick inspection of king snakes, rattlers, water moccasins, blue racers, and other Louisiana reptiles, all happily and safely stuffed, we were ready for some fresh air.

We headed for Jackson Square where my father sat on one of the benches under a magnolia tree and we chased the pigeons and ran around the statue of General Jackson. One day we read the inscription at the base of the statue "The Union must and shall be preserved." These words were put there, my father said, by General Benjamin "Spoons" Butler, the hated Yankee commander who headed occupation troops in the city during the Civil War. He was as dastardly a character, we thought, as Jackson was a heroic one. Butler earned his nickname "Spoons" from the fact that he confiscated so much silver from New Orleans households. My mother told us the story of how Butler also confiscated the stevedoring equipment owned by her grandfather Edmund Garland. Because he was at the time an English citizen, her grandfather was able to force Butler to pay for the equipment. But Butler made it so uncomfortable for him in New Orleans that he had to return to England for the rest of the war.

A more appealing character than Butler was Baroness Micäela Pontalba, the fiery Creole aristocrat who divorced her husband and was shot by her father-in-law---who then shot himself to death. These dramatic happenings we found more memorable than the fact that the baroness built the two beautiful apartment buildings flanking Jackson Square, or that she was the person responsible for transforming the square form a military parade ground to the lovely garden park we enjoyed so much.

Although the square was no longer the setting for marching militia or public executions, it had on display a strange and rather comic relic of the Confederate armed forces. This was a rusting iron submarine named the *Pioneer*. It was hard to convince us that this curious ungainly object, which looked like a giant metal fish, was used as a weapon in the Civil War. My father insisted that it had actually blown up a Yankee ship. This was an exaggeration I later discovered; it had merely blown up a barge, and on a practice run at that. The *Pioneer's* career came to an untimely end when it was scuttled and sunk in Lake Pontchartrain to prevent its falling into the hands of the Yankees when their troops occupied the city. It seemed to me that the Confederate Navy (like my father) had an exaggerated notion of the *Pioneer's* capabilities. The strange little vessel was later moved from a corner of Jackson Square to its present location under the arcade of the Presbytère.

When people came pouring out of the St. Louis Cathedral after the noon Mass, we sometimes went in for a quick visit. The Cathedral seemed dark and gloomy and not nearly as elaborate as I thought a cathedral was supposed to be. The Jesuit church on Baronne Street was more my idea of a cathedral. What impressed us most about the Cathedral was the burial place of Don Almonester y Roxas, under the church floor near the right side altar. Don Almonester, the Cathedral's great benefactor, provided funds for rebuilding the Cathedral after it was destroyed in the French Quarter conflagration of 1788. We always tiptoed quietly around the marble slab which bore Don Almonester's name and coat of arms.

Vying with Don Almonester for our interest was St. Anthony's Garden behind the Cathedral. This lovely little patch of green was once a favorite dueling spot for the city's hotheaded Creole gentlemen who crossed swords at a cross word---or less. My father said that New Orleans at one time had almost as many fencing masters and academies as Paris had. Creole men prided themselves on their fencing technique and demonstrated their expertise so often, while defending their honor, that the city sometimes had as many as three or four duels a day, often in St. Anthony's garden. Accustomed as we were to the swashbuckling adventures of Errol Flynn, Tyrone Power, Louis Hayward, and other heroes of the movies, we conjured up exciting scenes as we gazed through the iron fence enclosing the garden. Even then, however, I was struck by the irony of it all, men deliberately setting about to maim or kill each other just a stone's throw from where Mass was being celebrated in honor of Jesus Christ, the Prince of Peace. At least the last rites were close at hand when they were needed. I thought the pretty marble monument inside the garden, like an obelisk with a funerary urn on top, was there in memory of those who had fallen while defending their honor. I later found out that the names inscribed on the monument are those of thirty French sailors from the French frigate *Tonnerre* who died in the yellow-fever epidemic of 1857.

A few blocks down from the Cathedral at 1114 Chartres Street was the old Ursuline Convent, dating from 1745 and said to be be the oldest building in the Mississippi Valley. It is the only surviving structure from the French colonial period. The Ursuline nuns arrived in New Orleans from France in 1727, less than ten years after the city's founding. When they moved two miles below the city on North Peters Street in 1824, the convent on Chartres became a school for boys, a meeting place for the state legislature, and the home of the archbishop of New Orleans. As a child I knew it as the rectory of St. Mary's Italian Church. Today it is a museum and center for church archives.

The final stop on our Sunday morning expeditions to the Quarter was to the Morning Call for coffee and doughnuts, or beignets, as so many people refer to them today. I never heard the word beignet until I was an adult and a friend of mine from New York who was visiting New Orleans asked to go to the French Market for coffee and beignets. I didn't know what she was talking about. To us they were just doughnuts---not only a delicious treat, but lots of fun. All that powdered sugar! While the adults around us fastidiously corralled the snowy confection within their little orbit, we carefully timed our breathing so that we exhaled at just the right moment to propel a cloud of sugar onto our companions. Eventually we outgrew this type of behavior.

My visits to the French Quarter with my mother were very different from visits with my father. Mother occasionally went someplace in the Quarter to get scissors sharpened or umbrellas repaired or buttons covered. These errands were often extended into forays deeper into the Quarter where we would spend hours browsing through second hand furniture stores and curiosity shops, inspecting cut glass butter dishes and garnet jewelry. I knew the cut glass stock at Rau's on Royal Street intimately and only wish my mother had been a profligate buyer. At that time she thought that fifteen dollars for an ornate early American cut glass butter dish was outrageously overpriced. The only thing I remember her buying was a pretty, slender celery dish, which my sister Helen dropped and broke a few months later.

We sometimes walked as far as the Cabildo where Mother pointed out to us the apartment where she lived for a couple of years around the time of World War I. It was in a building behind the Cabildo known as El Calabozo, the site of the Spanish prison during colonial days. The building had been divided into two apartments and my mother's family lived upstairs in the apartment which had a balcony overlooking the courtyard of the Cabildo. She remembered the French Quarter as a residential neighborhood, very much like other neighborhoods, except that their playground was Jackson Square and instead of a nearby movie theater they had the French Opera House down the street. She said Pirates' Alley was then called Orleans Alley.

Sometimes when strolling the Quarter we'd pass some colored nuns leaving or returning to their convent at 717 Orleans Street. They were Sisters of the Holy Family (the order founded by Henriette Delille) and their three-story convent building had once housed the Orleans Ballroom, scene of quadroon balls where white Creole gentlemen met and danced with beautiful quadroon girls, and sometimes chose a mistress from among them.

Whenever we passed the vacant lot at Royal and St. Louis Street, Mother would tell us about the St. Louis Hotel, which had stood at that site and was demolished during the time she lived in the Quarter. She said it was the most beautiful building she had ever seen and she cried when the wreckers dismantled its spectacular copper plated dome. The hotel, built in 1841 (the first one built in 1837 was destroyed by fire) had been the scene of important social and civic functions and had served as the Louisiana state capitol for several years. The Royal Orleans Hotel now occupies the site.

If our errands in the Quarter were near Canal Street, we sometimes walked to the Custom House, a huge building which occupied the block bounded by Iberville Street, South Peters Street, Decatur Street and Canal Street. Here my mother would recount to us the story of how her grandfather solved the problem of delivering the marble used in the building's famous "marble hall."

It seems that when the ship carrying the marble arrived in port, local cargo handlers were afraid to extract the heavy marble from the ship's hold for fear of it falling and crashing through the deck. According to my mother, her grandfather, the one with the stevedoring company, devised a scheme for dismantling the deck; thereby allowing enough room for handling and safely hauling out the marble. Whether this is true or not, I have no idea; but the story has always made the Custom House a special New Orleans landmark for me. After it was refurbished a few years ago, I attended a reception there and was quite impressed with the "marble hall" which measures 128 feet by 84 feet and soars 58 feet high. It is constructed entirely of marble and iron. The Custom House stands on land that once formed the levee for the Mississippi River. (Since the founding of New Orleans the river has receded about four blocks to the east and many big buildings now stand on alluvial soil built up during the river's recession.)

Once in a while our neighbor Mrs. Buras and my mother went to the Farmer's Market at the French Market to buy bushels of vegetables and fruit which they divided. This was an exciting expedition and all of us kids were eager to go. We somehow squeezed the three Buras boys, Benny, Helen, me (and later our little brother Dan) and a couple of friends, plus the two adults into the Buras' four-door black Cheverolet. At that time Mother didn't drive and Mrs. Buras was the chauffeur for all of our outings. Before we went to the Farmer's Market we usually visited the seafood and meat stalls in the stucco buildings of the French Market. These structures with their arcades and columns were built in 1813 on the same site where Choctaw Indians used to trade with the early French settlers. Although there was a seafood stall at the LeBreton Market where we shopped every weekend, the extravagant displays of seafood at the French Market stalls were a special delight to the eye---as well as a shock to the nostrils. Besides the everyday varieties of seafood we were used to seeing at the LeBreton Market, there were octopus and squid, giant loggerhead turtles, tiny river shrimp, exotic fish like pompano and Spanish mackerel, and of course, huge metal cages filled with crabs and crawfish. There was stall after stall on each side of the building and we visited every one of them inspecting the specialities each had to offer. We made a short stop at the meat market where Mother bought some *chorice*, the hot sausage she used in making jambalaya.

Then we went to the arcade outside where the retail fruit and vegetable vendors had delectable displays of premium quality produce (at premium quality prices) and lovely bouquets of fresh-cut flowers. After an appreciative inspection of these goodies, we passed on to the open sheds of the Farmer's Market behind the seafood market where the produce was not so elegantly displayed but was much more reasonably priced. Mother and Mrs. Buras surveyed all the stands to determine the best buys. If we were lucky we saw some of the big trucks pull up and watched the farmers unload their crops. Watermelons were the most fun. The farmers piled the huge melons into little mountains of green elipses and then "plugged" a few on top, cutting out a triangular wedge to prove that their watermelons were really "red to the rind" as they loudly proclaimed them to be. When we found several to suit the demanding tastes of Mother and Mrs. Buras, the boys were commandeered to haul them to the car. Prospects of cold sliced watermelon mitigated the unpleasantness of this chore.

A completely different marketing experience from the noisy, helter-skelter atmosphere of the French Market was provided by a visit to Solari's, the elegant specialty food and spirits store at the corner of Iberville and Royal. Solari's was a New Orleans institution until it went out of business in the 1960s. As a special treat, after a doctor's or dentist's appointment in town, Mother would take me to Solari's to browse and have lunch. There was an open marble-topped lunch counter in the middle of the store and you could sit on a stool and watch the cooks and waitresses prepare and serve the food. The gumbo was almost as good as Mother made and the sandwiches were divine---fresh baked bread and cold cuts from Solari's delicatessen. We always took a tour of the store, buying a few delicacies, like olives and pickles from the giant barrels standing near the lunch counter, or fresh strawberries (better even than the ones at the French Market), orange slices from the candy counter, or macaroons from the bakery. We would sometimes go to the spirits department where my mother would consult Mr. Omer Cheer about what kind of wine to serve for Sunday dinner. Although we never bought more than one bottle of anything, he was always very polite and informative, using words like "dry" and "full-bodied", "fruity" and "smooth." We always seemed to wind up with a bottle of claret.

Later on, when I was working in the central business district I often stopped in Solari's for lunch, or to buy something special, or just to browse. They had a marvelous gift department with baskets and boxes of New Orleans goodies like Remoulade sauce, pralines, candied figs and strawberry preserves. I enjoyed sending gift packages from Solari's to out-of-town friends. I think my

fondness for the store stemmed partly at least from those enjoyable childhood visits.

I knew nothing about Bourbon Street when I was growing up. The only
time I found myself there was when I went in and out of the side entrance
to D. H. Holmes and Kreeger's or when Mother took me with her to Stewart's
Lighting Store in the 200 block of Bourbon where she bought lamps and had
them repaired. It wasn't until I was in college that I learned what Bourbon
Street was famous for.

I never noticed whether there were tourists in the French Quarter. The
people we saw seemed to be ordinary New Orleanians just like us, in the Quarter to shop or visit the Cabildo and Presbytère, or have coffee and doughnuts
at the Morning Call, or lunch at Arnaud's, Galatoire's, Antoine's or one of
the other famous French Quarter restaurants. There were no artists around
Jackson Square or Pirates' Alley and no jugglers performing in front of the
Cabildo. Occasionally we saw a "spasm" band of little Negro boys tap-dancing
and making a racket playing on home-made instruments of washboards, pot
covers, and tin cans. The Quarter was still primarily a residential neighborhood and many of the people we saw were residents going about their daily
business.

The French Quarter and Canal Street attracted New Orleanians from uptown and downtown and all around the town who satisfied their major shopping, entertainment, and business needs there. However, within our own
neighborhoods, we had a popular gathering place where, as children and teenagers, we spent a lot of our shopping and play time---our corner drugstore.

The Drugstore

When I was growing up, there was a drugstore in every neighborhood in New Orleans. Typically small family businesses located on a corner, the drugstores of that era were far removed in spirit, size, and merchandise from the supermarket drugstores of today.

Glass display cases lined their walls and checkered their tile floors. The wall cases, whose wood cabinets were often carved, inlaid or pedimented, were frequently as handsome as fine bookcases. Rising past whirring fans almost to the pressed tin ceiling they seemed to look disdainfully on the motley scene below. There a hodgepodge of drugstore paraphernalia was crammed together in seeming disorder. Jostling for floor space were such disparate objects as a standing scale, phone booth, magazine racks, pinball and bubble gum machines, lending library shelves and display cases filled with candy, cosmetics, stationery, tobacco products and the like.

But all of this exciting clutter paled before the splendor of the soda fountain, a temple of sweets that was the focal point of every drugstore. Backed by a huge mirror, bounded by swivel stools before a marble counter, and stocked with a glorious supply of ice cream, whipped cream, syrup, cherries and nuts, the soda fountain was the magnet that drew young people into the store. Such, indeed, was its popularity that its counter space was often flanked by booths or by marble-topped tables surrounded by bent-wire "drugstore" chairs.

But although the soda fountain was the drugstore's main attraction, the druggist's laboratory was its *raison d'être*. As children, however, we didn't realize this and would have been astounded if we had. In those days vile tasting medicine was the norm. Never swallowed without a fight, the mere mention of a dose could trigger pandemonium. Yet, as much as we hated medicine and kicked and screamed to prove it, we didn't equate it with the drugstore. A dose of castor oil and a sip of soda were, after all, light years apart. And since the druggist, in addition to his profession as a pharmacist, was usually the owner-operator of the store, it was in the latter role that we conveniently cast him.

Yet we sensed an air of mystery about the drugstore, something elusive that we couldn't put a finger on, but vaguely associated with the druggist's laboratory hidden away at the back of the store. This small, cavelike room was out of bounds to us and, therefore, fascinating. We had no idea how it looked inside or why the druggist so often disappeared into its depths. Nor could we fathom the musty odor that wafted through its door to permeate each nook and cranny of the store. We didn't dream that this mysterious odor was the scent of medicine in the making or, even worse, that our friend the druggist concocted the medicine we loathed.

On the contrary, we thought of the drugstore as a gingerbread house that brimmed with treats. There were take-out treats as well as sit-at-the-fountain treats. Of the former, hard penny candies, all day suckers, peppermint and licorice sticks, popsicles, Polar Bars and ice cream cones were the favorites. It was a grand thing as a child to be able to walk into the drugstore all alone, put down a penny or a nickel for a treat and then blissfully sucking or licking to wander freely through the neighborhood. This was the expedition I had in mind when at seven or eight I teased my mother to let me cross the street alone. When she finally relented, a whole new world opened up for me. Suddenly I was not only free of spirit, but also free to come and go, if not exactly as I pleased, at least to a satisfactory degree.

The childhood desire for treats was so great that a small friend and I once stooped to subterfuge to obtain them. My friend Jane was spending the day with me when this occurred. It was our nurse's day off and Mother had gone out for the afternoon putting us in the care of Rosie, the cook, and leaving us two nickels for a treat. But, to our distress, we lost the nickels, and Rosie, when applied to for a loan, said that she was broke. We found it necessary, therefore, to think of a moneymaking scheme. The one we finally hit upon was peddling soap in the neighborhood. Because we intended to begin with Rosie, hoping she was less broke than she said, we realized some sort of a disguise was necessary. And since Jane, in any case, would be less recognizable than I, she agreed to be the peddler. While I prepared her kit, several bars of soap packed into a shoebox, she stripped down to her little white petticoat, kicked off her sandals, stuffed cotton into her mouth and tied one of Daddy's handkerchiefs around her face. This startling metamorphasis erased the Jane I knew. In her place, I saw a little girl who had the mumps, an ailing mother, ten starving brothers and sisters, and a father who was out of work.

Sneaking out of the house, she rang the front doorbell. Rosie, however, proved resistant to her tale, still claiming lack of funds. But, as luck would have it, a chauffeur from around the corner happened to be passing by. He took pity on the "poor child" and bought two bars of soap for fifty cents. Upon receiving this windfall, Jane decided she had struck it rich and could, therefore, retire. Trying to get back into the house, she asked Rosie for a drink of water. But, fearful of the mumps on my account, Rosie led her through the driveway to the shed and gave her water in a jelly glass. At that point I ran out into the backyard and, in a fit of giggles, divulged Jane's true identity. Rosie, however, was not amused. Indeed, she took the fifty cents from Jane and vowed to give it to my mother. For it was Mother's soap, she said, that earned it. This was news to me for until then, I had assumed that everything in the house was as much mine as anyone's. At any rate, we didn't get a treat that day, but we did learn something about life and also about finances.

In a year or so, take-out treats gave way to sit-down treats at the fountain. The drugstore had, by then, become a meeting place, especially for small girls. Away from watchful eyes at home or school, we had a heady sense of freedom that made us feel almost grownup. Actually, there were other watchful eyes observing us, those of the druggist, the soda jerk (our hero), and other drugstore personnel. But most of the time we were oblivious to this. It was only when we were called down for unladylike behavior such as shouting, throwing straws, blowing bubbles in our sodas or noisily drawing their dregs, that we remembered we were children after all. Otherwise we revelled in our newfound freedom, happily indulging in sodas, sundaes, banana splits and malts. Each of these concoctions was as pleasing to the eye as to the palate, especially the banana splits that resembled frozen rainbows and the nectar sodas whose exquisite shade of pink made them blushing beauties. The sodas came in a variety of flavors and were always sipped through straws. Although they could be ordered plain, we usually opted for ice-cream sodas, for as yet we had no figures and, therefore, no calories to consider.

Here in New Orleans the star of every soda fountain was the nectar soda. A plain nectar soda was a glorious concoction made of simple syrup, vanilla and almond extracts, red food coloring and, of course, soda water. But when transformed into an ice cream soda by a scoop of vanilla ice cream and a cloud-like puff of whipped cream, it rivalled, at least for us, the nectar of the gods. It wasn't until later, however, that i realized the nectar soda was as charac-teristic of New Orleans as were *café au lait, café brûlot,* and the famous Sazerac cocktail.

When we were very young, the drugstore, in addition to being a sweet shop, took the place of a department store for us. Before we could go to Canal Street alone, we did our birthday and our Christmas shopping there. I can still remember how proudly I presented my parents with gifts I had selected on my own, usually cologne or chocolate covered mints for Mother and cigarettes or a bottle of lotion for Daddy. These modest gifts were always beautifully wrapped in white tissue paper or, at Christmas, green or red, for gift wrapping was done courtesy of the drugstore. Even the comic books I gave my little brother were gift wrapped, a bit of lagniappe that endowed them with a touch of class.

As we grew older, the use to which we put the drugstore changed. The soda fountain became a tempting place where boys and girls met with seeming nonchalance and eyed each other warily. Then, having made a conquest, they formed twosomes sipping single sodas through twin straws. Away from the soda fountain, drugstore furnishings that we had ignored in childhood sprang suddenly to life. The magazine rack became a mecca for girls mooning over movie magazines and boys guffawing over comic books. We girls also patron-ized the lending library, taking out romantic novels by the dozen. And, re-velling in our first flush of figure awareness, we put the standing scale to fre-quent use. The pinball machine was a favorite of the boys, its ringing bells and flashing lights mesmerizing them for hours. The phone booth, however, was popular with both contingents as a secluded spot for making private calls.

With the increased mobility of adolescence, the drugstore nearest home had strong competition from drugstores in other parts of town. On Saturday mornings streetcars converging on Canal Street disgorged herds of teenage girls on their way to a drugstore lunch and a movie. To be let loose on Canal Street minus chaperonage was a great adventure, one that made us feel we had, at long last, crashed the portals of the adult world.

When we learned to drive, curb service at the drugstore became the rage, especially on summer nights after the movies. It was great fun to pull up to the drugstore with a carload of girls or, even better, with a date. But the most fun of all was pulling up in a vintage car with a rumble seat or in a convertible with the top down. There was always a festive air about these curbside evenings. Music from the drugstore jukebox drifted out into the night, greetings were called from car to car, for even in a neighborhood that was new to us we seemed to meet old friends. Carhops, always male and dressed in gleaming white, dashed about taking orders and balancing aluminum trays that were especially designed to clamp on car doors. The orders on the trays, served with glasses of ice cold water, were not only perfect antidotes for a sweet tooth but also for the heat and humidity of a summer night. A particular favorite was one that required leaning out of the window for its consumption. This confection was a top-heavy triple decker ice-cream cone embellished by a quivering froth of whipped cream accented by a cherry.

On weekday afternoons the drugstore nearest school became a teenage rendezvous. When the dismissal bell rang, we stampeded there *en masse*. It was the "in" thing to see and be seen there, preferably puffing on a cigarette, and sipping a cherry or a lemon coke. For some obscure reason, cherry and lemon cokes, and especially the latter, were considered beverages of the worldly wise. With a lemon coke in one hand, a cigarette in the other and smoke rings seeping languidly from scarlet lips, it was easy to appear blasé, at least to one's confederates. Occasionally, however, the high spirits of adolescence broke through our studied pose. But even then we were careful to keep up a facade of propriety for we knew that under provocation the druggist was not above calling the school with a *résumé* of our behavior.

As I remember it, the drugstore was an ideal place for growing up. Removed from the pressures, restrictions, and nurturing of home and school, it was a secure, but neutral territory where, like children playing games, we could experiment with the trappings of maturity.

Rainy Days and Rubber Gun Wars

We had a favorite neighborhood drugstore too, but I don't think we spent much time there. We were too busy with other diversions, from playing marbles to waging rubber-gun wars.

We had a variety of chants and ditties for many of our games, some of them unique to New Orleans, like:

> "Ipson, dipson soda cracker,
> Does your father chew tobacco?
> Yes, my father chews tobacco,
> Ipson, dispon, soda cracker."

We used them when we were choosing up sides for a ball game or deciding who would be "It" for a game of Hide and Seek.

I'm always amazed at how little it took to amuse us when we were growing up. We could be entertained for days on end with a continuing game of monopoly or poker; besides team sports like baseball and softball, touch football and hockey (played on skates with palm branches and paper wads); we had marbles and yo-yos, tops and kites, paddleball and jacks, jump rope and hopscotch; there was skating and tennis, bike riding and swimming and fishing, even playing in the rain.

Many of these pastimes were the same ones being played by boys and girls all over the United States; but some had a New Orleans cachet, some even an esoteric neighborhood touch, that set them apart. For one thing we often used gris-gris in our game-playing, a custom emanating from the influence of voodoo in New Orleans.

103

The word gris-gris, presumably of African origin, means a charm, good or bad, but we used it exclusively as a hex against our opponents. We generally "put the gris-gris" on someone by pointing our fingers at them and giving them the "evil eye" (glaring ferociously). We took gris-gris quite seriously when we were little kids but as we got older we generally shouted "gris-gris" simply to unnerve our opponents.

I became disillusioned with gris-gris after an unfortunate attempt at playing marbles. Day in and day out, the game of marbles was probably the most popular pastime, especially among the boys. We called marbles "chinies" and our big marble shooters "boleys" or "aggies." I didn't know where these local names came from but New Orleans author and historian Charles L. "Pie" Dufour told me that "chinies" were so-called because they were made of china. Marbles were made of glass and "aggies" were made of agate. "Boleys" is a mystery.

Benny had a prodigious collection of "chinies" and "aggies," all of which he had won from other boys in our neighborhood. I could not resist the temptation one day to pilfer some of them, thinking to win a few games and parley Benny's "chinies" into a collection of my own. While I had had a dismal record as a marble shooter, I thought I had a secret weapon that was sure to make me a winner, a special gris-gris that our cook Beulah told me about. Beulah was our voodoo consultant and she convinced me that my gris-gris would be more powerful than anyone else's if I could point my fingers with the first joints turned down. This was not easy, but I practiced for several days until I could bend the first joint of the fingers of my left hand pretty easily and all but the little finger of my right hand. I decided that was good enough.

I went forth with my "borrowed" "chinies" and bent joints, confidently expecting to return home triumphant, replace Benny's "chinies" in their cigar box, and have a bunch left over for myself. I pointed my bent fingers at my opponent as he bent down to take aim at the "chinies" lined up in a banana-shaped ring. I pointed again and again as he proceeded to wipe me out, gleefully pocketing every one of Benny's "chinies" plus an "aggie" which I had also "borrowed." My defeat was particularly humiliating because my opponent was a "funky knuckle shooter." "Funky knuckle shooters" were considered easy marks by good marble shooters because they used a technique that was usually weak and ineffectual; they shot their agates off their thumb nails instead of their thumb knuckles.

I returned home and indignantly charged Beulah with the failure of her gris-gris. She burst out laughing. "You don't believe all that voodoo stuff, do ya?" she asked derisively. "That's a lot of *hoodoo*." She told me that some colored people who believed in voodoo made little dolls to put a spell on their enemies. They drank goat's blood and played with snakes. She said it was all a bunch of foolishness and she was making fun of voodoo when she told me about the bent fingers and the gris-gris. "Think they can scare *me* with that hoodoo?" she said, "just a lot of hooey." It was a long time before I put the gris-gris on anyone after that.

We played marbles, jump rope, jacks, and other games off and on all year round, but certain pastimes were seasonal. The long, hot summers provided endless hours for a variety of diversions, some of them special to New Orleans. One such was the rubber gun wars, waged intermittently all summer long. Soon after the close of school when I saw Benny begin to carve a piece of wood with a long snout, attach a clothes pin to the end of it, and cut strips from an old inner tube, I knew that war would soon be declared. Although this was primarily a boys' game, the tomboys of our neighborhood, including me, were allowed to take part in minor, back-up positions.

"My mother and your mother were hanging up clothes,
Your mother punched my mother right in the nose,
What color was the blood? R-E-D, red!"

These words rang out as the war leaders chose up sides for a battle. One summer Benny gave me one of his old rubber guns and I followed him around as he led his little group of fighters from one position to another up and down and around our block. Mostly I remember a lot of shouting, running from one yard to another, hiding behind fences and in garages, and shooting at other kids who were doing the same thing. After I got stung several times I lost my enthusiasm for rubber gun wars.

Another popular weapon was the pop-gun made from a piece of bamboo, with a wooden plunger whittled to fit the hollow of the bamboo. An empty spool made a perfect top for the plunger and an endless supply of ammunition was provided by numerous china ball trees, which bore berries just the right size and shape.

During times of truce we engaged in marathon games of monopoly or poker and hearts, and, because we were New Orleanians, we played for stakes.

As little kids we used match sticks and toothpicks as money, but as we grew older we played for pennies. We also played lotto, a kind of bingo game, with each player putting up several pennies for the pot. It was not unusual for us to continue these games for three or four days, sometimes even a week. We played on our front porch which was cooler than our un-air-conditioned house. We had oscillating fans and a big window fan in the house, which kept us reasonably comfortable at night, but merely blew hot air and our cards, paper money, and lotto markers all around during the day. Mother kept us fortified with pitchers of home-made root beer or lemonade and platters of sandwiches and cookies. On Saturdays my father, as a special treat, cooked us huge mounds of banana fritters or "lost bread" (stale bread soaked in a mixture of egg, milk, sugar and cinnamon, and deep fried).

We spent most of our summers outside, delightfully barefoot. Going barefoot was one of the nicest things about summer. We were constrained to rigid limits, however. We kept our shoes on until the last day of school, kicked them off and didn't put them on again (except for church-going and other dress-up occasions) until after Labor Day. We had similar rules for swimming. No matter how hot it got before the first day of June, we were not allowed to go swimming before June 1st, and we put away our bathing suits for the season the Tuesday after Labor Day. Mothers were convinced that we would all contract pneumonia or tuberculosis if we violated this ironclad rule.

Strangely enough, they had no qualms about our playing in the rain no matter what the season, even in the dead of winter.

> "Its's raining, it's pouring
> The old grey mare is snoring."

This sing-song chant was our rainy day ditty. I doubt if there was any other place in the country where kids usually greeted the onset of rain with shouts of "Oh, boy, it's raining!" Perhaps because it rained so much (New Orleans has an average annual rainfall of almost 60 inches) we figured we might as well enjoy it. If it was summer we quickly donned our bathing suits and dashed outside, lifted our faces to the sky catching raindrops in our mouths and sang out at the top of our lungs, "It's raining, it's pouring, the old grey mare is snoring." In winter we put on raincoat, hat, and galoshes, and sloshed around on the front lawn until our mothers finally made us come in. If there were a real cloudburst, which happened often enough, the gutters in our block filled to overflowing, and we had great fun wading through them and racing little home-made sailboats. Even better, when the streets flooded Benny launched his pirogue on the front lawn and we rowed aroung the neighborhood.

At least once during the summer a group of us threw a penny party, an idea we picked up no doubt from the annual school and church fairs in the neighborhood. This took a lot of organization and planning. First we collected all the throw-away trinkets and junk that our mothers would part with; then we made tickets out of construction paper, five cents admission, and we went all over the neighborhood selling them; then came the important part, planning and practicing the entertainment for the party. Benny and his friends constructed a makeshift stage for us in the backyard and Mother supplied an old bedspread for the curtain. We invited all the kids in the neighborhood to "audition" and then we selected the best ones to participate. At least that was the game plan. Actually, we took anyone brave enough to get on the stage. We knew that the more kids participated, the more parents and relatives would come and the more money we would make. We rounded up all the four, five, and six-year-olds in the neighborhood and gave them a crash course in singing, dancing, and elocution, using whatever knowledge and expertise we had absorbed from our own exposure to these "cultural" activities. Some of the performances were hilarious. I particularly remember one little boy's recital of:

> "The boy stood on the burning deck,
> His feet were full of blisters,
> When hark a lark, his drawers fell off,
> And now he wears his sister's."

We made grab-bags filled with trinkets and we sold refreshments, supplied by our mothers. We also raffled four or five cakes, again supplied by our mothers, for a penny a chance. As a finale we sometimes dressed in costume, decorated several wagons with crepe paper and had a Mardi Gras parade around the yard, throwing some of last year's Mardi Gras trinkets to our audience. There were so many of us involved in planning and managing the penny party that the division of profits from admission, sale of grab-bag items, refreshments, and raffles left each of us with about 50 cents. But we had been totally occupied and entertained for two weeks.

We often found amusements provided by nature in our own backyards.

Mosquito hawks, for instance. These graceful creatures descended on the city by the thousands during the summer months and their favorite resting places were backyard clothes lines. We loved to catch them and feed them tobacco which made them "drunk." Catching them required a special technique acquired through trial and error. Grabbing them by one set of wings was a mistake that I realized the first time I tried it. The mosquito hawk whipped around on my finger and grabbed me with its prickly legs and nipped me smartly. "Mosquito hawks can't bike," my mother said. But it felt like a bite to me. After that I sneaked up on them and grabbed a set of wings with the index finger and thumb of each hand. Holding them that way, it was easy to feed them a few strands of tobacco which they consumed as though they were on a lost weekend. Once released, they lost all sense of balance and floundered about looking like some of those ill-fated early flying machines; then, crash landing; followed by further tipsy attempts to take off and fly right. After a while the effects of the tobacco wore off and they gracefully ascended to the clothes line, then fluttered off, hopefully, to devour their daily quota of mosquitoes. Apparently, "mosquito hawk" is a regional (and aptly descriptive) name for these insects, whose real name is dragonfly.

Following the exodus of mosquito hawks and the onset of school right after Labor Day, fall and winter amusements took over, regulated by our school schedule and the weather. Skating, bicycling, hockey, touch football all had their turn on weekends and for an hour or so after school. The highlight of fall, however, was the Tulane University football games. Practically everyone in our neighborhood traveled up to Willow Street to Tulane Stadium on Saturday afternoons to cheer the Tulane Greenies. Our family was particularly enthusiastic because my father, who was a telegrapher, covered all the games for the Western Union, handling the play-by-play for the sports writers in the press box. He occasionally got a pass for Benny to accompany him. In those days, the press box was for men only and I was never allowed to go. I didn't care though. I loved sitting in the End Zone with all my friends, jumping up and down and joining in the cheers. We went wild when the Tulane cheerleaders came to our section to lead us in the touchdown cheer:

> "Hullabaloo, ray, ray
> Hullabaloo, ray ray
> Hooray, hooray,
> Vars, vars, T-Ay

T - Ay, T - Ay, Vars Vars T - Ay
Tulane!"

The end zones, jammed with children and teenagers, held as much activity as the football field itself. The younger kids spent the entire afternoon running up and down the steps and in and out of the aisles pursuing popcorn and coke vendors, consuming untold quantities of junk, throwing paper wrappers at one another, playing hide and seek and occupying themselves with anything but watching the game. Half of them didn't know the score when the game was over; some of them probably didn't even know who won. I usually studied the football program carefully, picked out the best-looking players and watched them the entire game. Tulane Stadium, dormant for several years after the Superdome was built, was demolished in 1980.

A special treat for several winters was the appearance of the Ice Capades in New Orleans. This traveling ice production probably visited cities all over the country but it's unlikely that it was as enthusiastically received anywhere else as it was in semi-tropical New Orleans where snow and ice were such rarities. The Ice Capades provided one of the great thrills of our growing-up years. Even more thrilling than the show itself, which everyone agreed was spectacular, was our own attempt at ice skating; for the Ice Capades Company rented skates to the public after each performance and at other times during their two-week stint at the Municipal Auditorium. Sonja Henie was at the height of her movie career then, so besides the novelty of the ice itself there was the added allure of Hollywood glamour attached to ice skating. For the boys, mastering the skates was the challenge; for the girls it was trying to look like Sonja Henie. Whatever our motives, we all had a rude awakening the first time we ventured onto the ice. There was only a split second between placing our feet in the rink and landing flat on our bottoms. However, a handsome young instructor came over to me the first time, helped me to my feet and guided me around the rink. I began to get the hang of it, or so I thought, until he let me go and I sailed right to the edge of the ice, not knowing how to stop myself, and fell into one of the rinkside seats. After several more sessions with the instructor I managed to stay up for a few seconds at a time. Just when I began to feel confident, however, I saw one of my friends take a spill. I started laughing and fell on the ice beside her. By the time we were ready to go home we were as wet as if we'd been swimming instead of ice skating, but eager to return to the Auditorium for another try. We hated to see the Ice Capades leave town and eagerly awaited their return the following year.

Except for skating at the Ice Capades, the only exposure I had to "northern" winter sports as a child occurred during a rare snowfall in New Orleans when I was in the second grade. We went to school as usual that morning of the snow, and little flurries began to fall even before we got into our classrooms. Pandemonium broke loose, particularly when it became apparent that our teachers were just as excited about this unusual phenomenon as we were. We were given early recess and spent our time collecting enough snow off the ground to make snowmen. The older children were busy throwing snowballs and trying to make sleds from pieces of wood they got from the manual training instructor. Suddenly someone shouted and pointed up. We turned and our gaze reached the roof of our school building, where an amazing scene greeted our eyes. There were our teachers shouting, jumping up and down, and throwing snowballs at one another. Some of them were even throwing snowballs down at *us*. This extraordinary behavior was more surprising to me than the snowfall. Shortly thereafter, our stern and formidable principal Miss Limmer (who did *not* appear on the roof) announced that the rest of the day was a holiday. It didn't snow again in New Orleans, not noticeably anyway, for more than twenty years.

We grew up in an era of contests, held intermittently all year round, contests for shooting marbles, spinning tops, flying kites, kicking footballs, catching fish, even collecting tin foil. We lived from one contest to the next. The one I remember most vividly was a yo-yo contest.

One day excitement flew through our neighborhood as word spread that a real, live Japanese yo-yo champion was coming to New Orleans to conduct a contest. (The Japanese were supposed to be the best in the world.) He was going to award prizes for the best performers. Everyone searched out his or her favorite yo-yo and began practicing like crazy. We practiced on our way to school, during recess and lunchtime, on our way home from school and all weekend. Finally, one Saturday morning the Japanese champion did show up, at the Bell movie theater, and we all lined up in front of the show to display our well-practiced techniques.

The champion first gave a demonstration. After seeing what he could do with a yo-yo, we all felt like going home and calling it a day. He could not only make his yo-yo "sleep" and "walk the dog," "go around the world" and "rock the baby," he could do things with that yo-yo we could never have imagined. He was like a magician, keeping it in constant motion, swinging, twisting, spinning, circling, all the while looking at us and smiling broadly. He was almost as much a curiosity as his yo-yo. We had never seen a Japanese before, except in newsreels where they were usually shown dropping bombs on the Chinese.

We finally got up enough courage to display our feeble talents. Surprisingly, the champion considered Benny and a couple of other boys adept enough to be awarded a free championship yo-yo. He assured the rest of us that our skills would definitely improve if we went out and bought one of those special models. This claim, needless to say, was greatly exaggerated.

All the games and sports and pastimes I have talked about were things we did on weekdays and Saturdays. Sunday was different. It was a special day of the week and our Sunday activities were not the same as those of other days. I think this was true whether you lived downtown or uptown.

Sunday

The Sundays of my childhood were dramatically different from other days of the week. Although Sunday was a holiday, it was also a holy day and faithfully observed as such.

At our house, breakfast was, as usual, first on the agenda. But it was a breakfast with a difference. On weekdays my brother and I endured breakfasts that were good for us, but on Sundays we enjoyed a breakfast that was good. On her way to work, Rosie, our cook, stopped at a bakery for the sweetrolls that were its main and only course. Far removed from weekday oatmeal, they were frosted with icing, studded with raisins, which I didn't like and methodically removed, and accompanied by cups of steaming *café au lait*. For Brother and me, however, the *café au lait* was only ten percent coffee and ninety percent milk, as opposed to half and half for the adults. Nevertheless, it was a treat, for Sunday morning was the only time we were allowed to drink it.

After breakfast, Daddy divided the Sunday paper, allotting the funnies to Brother and me, and we all settled down to read. Mother, Daddy and Grandpa stayed at the table, but Brother and I took the funnies to the sitting room, spread them on the floor and, lying on our stomachs, proceeded to devour them. Brother was an ardent fan of Popeye, his girlfriend Olive Oyl, and their cohort Alice the Goon, but my favorites were Maggie and Jiggs, with Winnie Winkle as a runner up. When Brother finished reading first, he whirled away the time with his imitation of the goonish Alice. Prancing about with fiendish glee, he clowned until I erupted and a sibling fight ensued. This broke the Sabbath peace and inevitably evoked a summons from the dining room. Happily, however, the hall clock often chimed at just about this time and we were dismissed, minus punishment, to get ready for Mass.

There was nothing casual about churchgoing in those days, for Sunday services were not only religious ceremonies but also formal occasions. Indeed, it was the custom for families to go to church together, dressed up in their Sunday best. It was also customary to carry a thick black Bible, Missal or prayerbook to church. As a child, however, I carried a Missal with a Mother-of-Pearl cover and a filigree gold clasp. This was very much to my liking, for the wearing of Sunday finery heightened my enjoyment of the day. Vain to the core, I imagined that all eyes were upon me as I walked up the aisle in my pretty frock, saucy hat, short white cotton gloves and black patent leather Mary Janes. Brother, however, saw things in a different light and objected strenuously to dressing up. Yet he always looked angelic in his little sailor suit.

The Mass we attended was over by noon, a time when all the church-bells in the city seemed to be ringing, either tolling the hour, pealing the Angelus, or chiming to mark the end of services. As we drove home amidst this cacophony of sound, we were treated to the sight of fashionably dressed congregations pouring from the churches along St. Charles Avenue. All of the women wore hats, smart little felts in winter and wide brimmed straw cartwheels from Easter until the first cool snap of fall. The men, depending on the season, wore straw boaters or felt fedoras, but boys usually went bareheaded and small girls often passed up a hat for a ribbon or a big butterfly bow. In cool weather, many of the women wore a fox fur draped around their shoulders. This furpiece fascinated Brother, for it presented the unfortunate fox in its entirety, from head to bushy tail. It also fascinated me, but for a different reason. I looked forward to the time when I, too, would wear one. But, alas, when that time came, the tables had turned in favor of the fox and it was no longer fashionable.

Upon arriving home we sat down to a big Sunday dinner. As a child, I found this dinner as exciting as a party for, in addition to its topsy-turvy timing, it was a big production. The table was decked out in full regalia and the meal itself was a feast. The menu invariably revolved around a chicken or a roast. We could always expect to have rice and gravy, but the other dishes changed with the seasons. Baked yams and candied cushaws were featured in the fall, strawberry shortcake in spring-time, creamed turnips in the dead of the winter, and stewed okra, Creole tomatoes and homemade ice cream all summer long.

Making ice cream was a Sunday morning ritual. It was also a big event, for it was Mother's only culinary venture. Brother and I hovered near while she prepared the custard and Rosie chipped ice from the huge, fifty-pound block in the ice box. When the custard was made, Mother ladled it into the freezer can, then gave us the big yellow bowl to scrape. At this point, Rosie took over. After putting the dasher in and securing the cover, she carried the can to the back porch, placed it in a wooden pail and packed crushed ice around it. Brother and I watched impatiently, for it was our job to turn the crank. We always started turning with great gusto. But Rosie took a dim view of our speed. "Whoa, slow down!" she would exclaim, "Don't you know slow turnin' makes smooth ice cream?" Before long, we had no choice, for the turning became difficult and, finally, impossible. When this happened we knew the ice cream was frozen. This meant it was time to lick the dasher. Hooray!

Every Sunday the ice cream was a different flavor. We had vanilla ice cream made with real vanilla beans, peach ice cream laced with golden peach slices and strawberry ice cream with some of the berries still delectably whole. Mother also made banana ice cream, lemon milk sherbert, and frozen cream cheese, using Creole cream cheese, of course. And after Easter she transformed any chocolate rabbits that were still intact into the best chocolate ice cream I have ever tasted.

Mother's ice cream was so good, I sometimes wondered why she didn't try her hand at something else. But eventually I realized this was Rosie's doing. For Rosie had long since claimed the kitchen for herself, declaring it off limits to the adults of the family. Yet, for some obscure reason, she allowed Mother into her domain for the Sunday morning ritual of making ice cream.

Rosie never tired of telling Brother and me how she had "raised" mother and our uncles and had known Daddy when he was a young boy. "They all use to call me Mammy, same as you do." She would tell us. "But they too big to call me Mammy now." Woe betide Brother and me, however, if we dared to call her anything else.

Rosie was a martinet---no doubt about it---but it was plain to see she had a heart of gold. Brother and I loved Rosie. We also loved Mary, our nurse. But Rosie fascinated us, for like the Fig Woman who passed our house on summer days, she had star quality.

After Sunday dinner we sometimes went to Audubon Park or to a neighbor-

hood movie. More often, however, we piled into the car for a drive in the
country. Our favorite route was along the River Road, upriver towards Baton
Rouge. As Daddy maneuvered the winding road, the grassy mound of the
levee kept pace with us like a green ribbon rolled out beside the car. Drifts
of buttercups and clover tumbled down its banks, cows grazed there and an
occasional horseback rider galloped by. Now and then, a ship's mast rose
above the levee's crest as if to remind us that the river, though unseen, was
really there. To our right, vegetable patches hugged the road and, beyond
them, fields of sugarcane fanned out as far as we could see. From time to
time, the flat landscape was punctuated by a church, a tiny fenced-in cemetery, or a country store with a lone gas pump before it. The houses along
the way were few and far between. Now and then we passed a weather-beaten
cabin with a washing machine on the front porch or a white clapboard bunga-
low nestled in a pretty garden. But I was on the lookout for the manor houses
of the vast plantations that once lined the river between New Orleans and
Baton Rouge. Mother and I were hopelessly in love with them, and Daddy,
tolerant of our infatuation, slowed down or stopped at the first glimpse of
white columns peeping through an avenue of trees.

Mother was intrigued by the history and architecture of the houses, but
I romanticized them. Roaming in my imagination through their spacious rooms
and on their pillared galleries, I peopled them with companions of my choice
and made up stories of my own. My favorite plantations were Houmas House
and Uncle Sam, the latter since claimed by the river. It was a rare treat, however, when I saw them, for both were miles beyond our usual drive. Houmas
House was the quintessential antebellum mansion. Surrounded by Doric columns and shaded by live oaks festooned with Spanish moss, it was, although
still occupied, as mysterious to me as Sleeping Beauty's castle. Paradoxically,
Uncle Sam, then in its twilight years, unoccupied and seemingly abandoned,
retained a strong life force that made it fascinating. Unlike the other plantation houses that we passed, it remained the hub of a complete group of
plantation buildings---*garçonnières, pigeonniers*, an office and a kitchen that
resembled tiny temples, and, in the distance, slave quarters and a huge sugar-
house.

Our drives along the Mississippi abruptly changed to cruises on Lake
Pontchartrain when Daddy bought a boat. This shift of scenery suited Daddy
and Brother to a "T" but it took a while for Mother and me to forget our
plantation love affair and fall for the attractions of the lake. I'll never for-

get the first time I saw the boat. I was ten years old and it was Christmas day. Mother and Daddy revolutionized our schedule by taking us to early Mass and, afterwards, for a mysterious drive to the lakefront. On arriving at West End, Daddy pulled up to the Yacht Club Pen and suggested that we all take a walk on the pier. It was unusually cold that Christmas and our teeth chattered as we walked past rows of pleasure boats berthed in narrow slips. Suddenly Daddy stopped before a sleek white cabin cruiser, said "There she is!" and motioned us aboard. Bursting with curiosity, we followed him into a panelled saloon where a little Christmas tree blazed with colored lights. "Merry Christmas!" Daddy said. Then he and Mother, their eyes dancing, beamed at us expectantly. We erupted into whoops and hollers. This was the best Christmas we had ever had!

In those days, there was no marina on the lakefront. Pleasure boats were berthed in the New Basin Canal, where the neutral ground of Pontchartrain Boulevard is today, or in the Yacht Club Pen. To reach the lake from the pen, we had to signal the keeper of the bridge between the pen and basin that we wanted to come through. Daddy did this by setting off the banshee wail of the boat's siren. Then, while waiting for the bridge to open, Brother and I waved to everyone in sight---people in cars halted by the rising bridge, other boat people, pedestrians on a nearby footpath and, as we passed beneath the bridge, the bridgekeeper himself, in his little windowed cubicle. Once in the basin, we took a left turn and Lake Pontchartrain was straight ahead.

I always felt a surge of joy as we swept from the basin into the open water of the lake. Since the far shore was invisible, it was easy to imagine that we were on an ocean voyage to exotic lands. Our nearest brush, however, with anything exotic was the amusement park at Pontchartrain Beach. As we approached it, the "wildcat," or scenic railway, loomed before us like an enormous cut-out pasted against the sky. Then, as we drew nearer, the garish mechanical rides and refreshment stands of the midway came into focus and the blare of music and the shrieks of "wildcat" riders floated out to us across the water. But, despite its tantalizing proximity, Pontchartrain Beach was an elusive never-never land. For, as small children, Brother and I never set foot on it but were only rowed into its shallow waters for a swim.

Sometimes we cruised to the bridges, one for trains, the other for cars, that spanned the lake's narrow eastern end, approximately five miles wide. Once there, we dropped anchor and, rocking gently, watched the Sunday fishermen trying their luck from the wooden pilings of the railroad bridge. Occasionally we set a northerly course parallel to the bridges, crossed the lake and cruised into the placide waters of Bayou Liberty. There, the sharp, clean scent of pines, the sight of cypress trees, their knobby knees breaking through the shallows, and the pastoral beauty of the countryside left us in no doubt that we were on a "foreign" shore. Although we seldom fished in the lake, we always fished in Bayou Liberty, bringing our catch to friends who had a summer place nearby. Their house, like many along the bayou, was an old-fashioned clapboard structure circled by screened porches. It was set in a glade of magnolias, pines, and live oaks and surrounded by mammoth azalea and camellia bushes and a wide lawn that swept down to the water. But best of all, it had a swimming pool! Brother and I, raring to jump in, were always in our bathing suits when we tied up at the dock.

Although we enjoyed going to Bayou Liberty, our trips there were few and far between. We usually spent Sunday afternoon cruising on the lake. Perched on the foredeck, Brother and I watched the other boats that were out for a spin or a sail, peering at them to see if we knew anyone on board, but waving willy-nilly. We also scanned the shoreline for familiar landmarks. The camps and piers of Little Woods, the gleaming Coast Guard lighthouse, the distant skyline of the city, Pontchartrain Beach and Shushan Airport, now New Orleans Airport, were all identified enthusiastically. But the Southern Yacht Club, the second oldest yacht club in the nation, was our favorite. Still a landmark at the mouth of the New Basin Canal, it is now a modern structure, but then it rose above the skyline like a giant wedding cake. A multi-tiered frame building surrounded by screened porches, crowned with a cupola and built on pilings above the water, it was our haven when a sudden squall blew up and Daddy decided not to take the boat out. Even in the wildest storms, the club house, though lashed by waves, was safe and snug. Brother and I loved to watch the fury of the storm from the safety of its screened porch while pretending we were riding the high seas in a great ocean-going vessel. We also amused ourselves by sliding on the polished ballroom floor or looking at the myriad nautical photographs that lined the lobby walls. But when I had a female friend in tow, we sometimes left Brother to his own devices and slipped into the chintzy, wicker-furnished ladies lounge to primp and preen before the dressing table mirrors.

Since Rosie had the evening off, we always stopped at a delicatessen for supper supplies after our Sunday afternoon outings. The day thus ended as it had begun, with a meal that was different from its weekday counterparts.

I thoroughly enjoyed those Sunday suppers. The combination of a guest or two, a casual table setting and picnic fare such as cold cuts, pickles, potato salad and deviled eggs endowed them with the pleasant informality of alfresco meals. But, except in summertime, gloom set in soon afterwards. For the next day was Monday and, for nine months of the year, that meant only one thing---school.

Lake Pontchartrain

Look at the map of New Orleans and you will notice that the city hugs Lake Pontchartrain on one side and the Mississippi River on the other. When I was growing up, the river was almost a stranger to us, but the lake was an old and comfortable friend. It played an important role in the recreational and social lives of New Orleanians of all ages and from all parts of the city.

We used the lake for a variety of diversions---swimming, fishing, crabbing, boating, dining, picnicking, and excursions along its winding shoreline, which stretched for miles from West End eastward to the Industrial Canal. Some New Orleanians kept boats moored at the pen at West End near the Southern Yacht Club. The Club, established in 1849, was an elegant setting for high-school and college dances. Protruding from the shore about six miles east of West End was the New Orleans Airport (originally Shushan Airport) where we could watch planes take off and land, something of a novelty in those days. One of my own favorite lakefront spots was Pontchartrain Beach, the giant amusement park at Elysian Fields and the lake, which was the setting for our annual family picnics.

The lake figures importantly in the history and development of New Orleans. It was a vital link in the city's founding, for its waters connected the area with the Gulf of Mexico (via Lake Borgne) and the French colonial settlements along its coast.

The shoreline of the lake looks a lot different today than it did to those early explorers and colonists. For one thing the shore is actually 3,500 feet further into the lake now than it was then and it has a concrete seawall along its banks instead of a swampy morass. During the 1930s the Works Progress

Administration drained the lakeshore and filled it with sand dredged from the lake. The subsequent beautification program transformed the whole lakefront area into a recreational park.

However, the lakefront had a long history of recreational facilities before that, as far back as the early eighteen hundreds when an elegant hotel and resort flourished at Spanish Fort, located at the junction of Bayou St. John and the lake. About a mile east of Spanish Fort was Milneburg, a settlement founded by philanthropist Alexander Milne. When the Pontchartrain Railroad began its five-mile run from Elysian Fields in the Faubourg Marigny to Milneburg in 1832, the area opened up as a summer resort. New Orleanians began building vacation "camps" along the lakeshore. "Camps" were simple cottages built on stilts over the water.

The only thing left of old Milneburg (which everyone pronounced "Milenburg") is a lighthouse which was built in 1855. The lighthouse also survived the recent demise of the Pontchartrain Beach amusement park. The park was built on the Milneburg site in the 1930s and was the favorite of all our picnic spots. Whenever I see the lighthouse I remember the day Helen climbed to the top of it, causing excitement and apprehension up and down the Pontchartrain Beach boardwalk. (Prior to its location at Milneburg, Pontchartrain Beach operated for several years at the junction of the Lake and Bayou St. John).

We had three or four all-day picnics at the amusement park each summer, teaming up with another family for the long trek from Gentilly Blvd. out to the lake. Benny, Helen, and I scurried about doing odd jobs several days ahead of time earning money for our anticipated fling in the Penny Arcade. The Arcade was a popular attraction, with its baseball and football game machines, fortune-telling mechanical gypsy, movie machines, pinball machines, and best of all, slot machines. Our mother supplied funds for us to ride the amusements along the boardwalk but not for the slot machines and games in the Penny Arcade. Besides our odd jobs, we raised money by getting Mother to bake a cake which we raffled to other kids in the neighborhood for a penny a chance.

On the morning of the picnic everyone was up at the crack of dawn, packing bathing suits, towels, tablecloths, beach balls, and most important of all, food. The smell of frying chicken and *"panné"* meat (fried breaded round steak) filled the house; that was standard picnic fare. Mother also made potato salad, cookies, and sometimes a three-layer coconut cake to take along.

Down the street the Buras family, our traditional picnic companions, was going through the same preparations. I always sneaked over to their house to watch Mrs. Buras' mother make potato chips, one of their contributions for the day. They were really soufflé potatoes, I suppose, but that was before I knew anything about the menu at Antoine's or Galatoire's. At that time I thought it was absolute magic to be able to make potato chips in your own kitchen. Mrs. Bouchet used two big iron pots filled with hot oil, dumping the thinly sliced potatoes from one pot to the other and they would fluff up "like magic." She drained them on a piece of brown paper bag, lightly sprinkled them with salt, and then packed them in another big paper bag for the picnic. She never minded if a few of them disappeared between one paper bag and the other. Needless to say, potato chips have never tasted the same since.

When every possible preparation had been completed, we finally piled into the Buras' car and headed out to the lake. When my little brother Dan entered our family, when I was ten years old, we had to pack, along with everything else, a stroller and a baby mattress and blanket for him. I never remember fathers going on those picnics; they probably considered picnics above and beyond the call of duty.

During the ride to the lake we were bombarded with instructions and admonitions. We had to promise not to fight with each other, not to talk to strangers, not to go too far out into the lake while swimming. We were told about sharks and deep holes and currents which carried you all the way across the lake to Mandeville. We were to report back to picnic headquarters every half hour. If not heard from in more than an hour the police would be notified. The younger children were forbidden to go on the Wildcat (the roller coaster later known as the Zephyr) and the older ones were instructed to see that their safety bar was properly secured and not by any means to try to stand up or try any other daredevil tricks while on any of the rides. The length of the instructions always seemed to last the length of the trip from home to the beach.

Finally we arrived and had to curtail our itch to be off and running until all the supplies were unloaded and our picnic site staked out. This was usually under an overhang close to the flying horses. We were given our one dollar each and told to make it last all day. We were off in a flash. The rides were ten cents so we had to reconnoiter the boardwalk and make careful calculations and decisions about how to allocate our funds. We picked out

our favorite rides and decided the order in which to enjoy them, saving the
best for last. The boys usually rode several times on the bumper cars, competing to see who could ram the most cars. They were sometimes reprimanded
by the ride operator for being too competitive and causing huge jam-ups in
the middle of the rink. I stayed away from the bumper cars and spent most
of my money on the Bug and the Airplanes. All of us went on the Laugh-
in-the-Dark at least once and if we were old enough we rode the Zephyr just
to show how brave we were. I secretly hated it. Between rides we strolled
along the boardwalk and watched people trying their hand at different skill
and chance amusements, throwing baseballs at iron milk bottles; tossing pennies at numbered squares; aiming darts at balloons tacked to a wall. Benny
spent some of his money at the shooting gallery. The gallery made a terrific
racket, with the banging of the guns, the creaking of the constantly moving
duck decoys and the twang of an occasional hit.

We always cherished the hope that we could parlay some of our pennies
into a bankroll by playing the slot machines in the Penny Arcade. One summer I won the jackpot in the penny slot machine, $5.00 in pennies came tum-
bling out and every kid in the place scrambled for a piece of the action. Benny
got the lion's share and generously returned almost all of it to me.

The day I won the jackpot I was on my way back to picnic headquarters
with my pennies in my bathing cap when I noticed a big crowd standing by
the Lighthouse. Everyone was looking up. I looked up too and saw two
small figures at the window at the top of the Lighthouse. They were looking
down, smiling and waving. After a few seconds I realized that they were my
sister Helen, then seven years old, and her bosom buddy, Gilbert Buras, also
seven. There was a lot of noise, people exclaiming and pointing, and then
I saw Mrs. Buras wringing her hands. And next to her stood Mother, crying.
Everyone was shouting: "Come back down, you kids!," "Don't come down!,"
"Wait for the lighthouse keeper," "Be careful!" Just then the guard, at any
rate someone in uniform, arrived, muttering "How did those kids get up there?"
As he went to the back of the lighthouse, I followed him and saw him open
a little door and go in. I peeked inside and caught my breath. The narrow
circular interior was dark and forbidding and the open metal stairway spiral-
ing up to the top was old and treacherous looking. (The lighthouse had gone
out of service in 1929). The guard shouted up to Helen and Gilbert not to
touch any wires, not to come down alone and not to move at all until he came
up to carry them down, which he promptly did. He had a problem with Gil-

bert, however, who refused to cooperate until his mother promised not to
spank him when he reappeared. Finally they were both returned to irate but
grateful mothers, and Gilbert and Helen were the talk of the neighborhood
for weeks afterward.

Swimming was an important part of every picnic. We spent a couple of
hours in the lake before lunch. My mother always followed us to the beach
under her umbrella to keep track of us and shouted frantically when she thought
we strayed out too far. After swimming we had an extended lunch and since
we were not allowed back in the water for two hours after eating, we headed
back to the Penny Arcade and the rides.

The most exhausting part of the day for our mothers was probably the
final round-up. No one wanted to go home. Collecting all the children and
re-loading all the supplies was an extended trial. One kid was sent to fetch
the others, only to disappear himself. That continued until the ultimate threat
was issued, no more picnics unless everyone reported pronto!

Picnics at Pontchartrain Beach were our favorites but we had smaller,
less adventurous ones at West End. There was a small strip of beach there
right off the seawall near the Coast Guard station and the lighthouse across
from the Southern Yacht Club. Unlike Pontchartrain Beach, there were no
amusements or concessions at West End, just a nice beach for swimming, sun-
ning and picnicking.

Part of the fun of those picnics was in getting there, via the West End
streetcar along the New Basin Canal. What a ride that was! The New Basin
Canal lay between Pontchartrain Boulevard and West End Boulevard and our
eyes were glued to the ever changing scene on the canal as our streetcar charged
out West End Boulevard toward the lake, furiously swaying from side to side
and screeching to a halt at little covered way stations on the route. The stations were lined with benches and resembled the ends of waterfront piers,
like the ones we knew on the Gulf Coast. We saw people fishing from the
stations and along the banks and an occasional group of boys in swimming,
although the water was covered with splotches of oil and gunk. There were
all kinds of craft in the canal, oyster luggers, barges hauling bricks, sand, coal
and gravel, skiffs and other fishing boats, pleasure boats, and an occasional
sailboat. We turned our heads from the canal scene now and then to watch
for the house with the blue roof on West End Boulevard. This was the most
outstanding landmark on the boulevard and we competed to see who would
spot it first.

The one mile and two mile Southern Amateur Athletic Union swimming races were held each summer in the New Basin Canal. When we were old enough, Helen and I participated in them. Again we watched for the house with the blue roof, this time from the water. Helen won both races several years in a row. I was lucky to finish them. The canal was dirty and scary to swim in. Once I mistook a floating log for an alligator. (At least everyone assured me after the race that I was mistaken.) When we emerged from the water our faces were so dirty we looked as though we belonged in a minstrel show.

The New Basin Canal was the brainchild of some uptown American businessmen and was designed to compete with the Carondelet Canal in the downtown Creole sector. It was dug by hand (mostly Irish immigrant hands) during the 1830s and was filled in in 1950 to make way for the Pontchartrain Expressway. It originally ran six miles from the lake to a turning basin at South Rampart Street between Julia Street and Howard Avenue near the present Union Passenger Terminal and Greyhound Bus Station.

When I was in high school and college Spanish Fort was a favorite spot for picnics and hayrides. It had long been abandoned as an amusement park and resort, but the old fort's crumbling brick walls and neat picnic grounds still attracted visitors. The fort started out as a meager fortification erected by the French and known as Fort St. Jean. It was rebuilt and enlarged by the Spanish after they took possession of Louisiana in 1769 and became Fort San Juan. It was manned during the War of 1812, but in its lifetime the fort never came under attack and its cannons never fired a shot. The land was sold to private investors in 1823 and Spanish Fort enjoyed great success as a resort off and on for almost one hundred years. At one time it had a bathing pier that extended one mile into the lake and had tracks that shuttled people back and forth for a nickel fare. Celebrities who visited the resort included Oscar Wilde, who lectured there, and William Makepeace Thackeray and General Ulysses S. Grant, who dined there.

It was near Spanish Fort that voodoo queen Marie Laveau practiced bizarre rites every year on St. John's Eve, June 23rd. Even before her time the bayou had been a favorite meeting place for practitioners of the voodoo cult, which was a mixture of African animism, witchcraft, superstition and, in the case of Marie Laveau, a touch of Christianity. Her voodoo rituals attracted not only her cult followers but large crowds of curious onlookers attracted by tales of wild, obscene dancing and animal sacrifice.

Midway between Spanish Fort and West End was Benny's favorite place to go shrimping off the seawall. Several times during the summer, my father took us on night-time excursions to the lake just to cool off and Benny would bring along his cast net and a bucket for the catch. (He was always an optimist when it came to fishing or shrimping.) Time and again he would cast out and empty the contents of his net on the seawall steps. Helen and I had great fun scooping up the shrimp, which had amazing powers of locomotion, and transferring them to the bucket. Occasionally one would leap from our grasp and wind up back in the lake, much to Benny's disgust.

When we tired of shrimping, my father would take us on a spin around West End Park to admire the colored fountain before heading for home. It seems strange nowadays that a fountain with changing colors would be such an attraction, but there was always a crowd at West End to see it and a steady stream of cars making the circle around the park. I remember the acute disappointment I felt the first time we went out there and the fountain wasn't working. It still stands in the middle of the park, unused and dilapidated, perhaps waiting for some re-awakening when its magic lights will again bring some moments of enchantment and delight to passersby.

Once or twice a year Mother and Dad took us to one of the restaurants at West End. Fitzgerald's was my favorite. I loved crossing the little bridge to get to the entrance and then sitting at a window looking right over the water. More than a century ago West End was a booming resort with a hotel, bathhouses, amusement park, a scenic railway built over the water, a bandstand, pavilion and theaters. The city's first movies were shown there in 1896, on a canvas screen set up in front of the bandstand. This all disappeared when the city built the West End seawall and the thirty-acre West End Park in 1921.

A little west of West End, just on the other side of a rickety but picturesque wooden bridge was the little fishing village of Bucktown with boat moorings in the 17th Street canal on one side of the street and camps over the lake on the other side. It doesn't have as many camps now but still looks very much the way I remember it as a child. (The bridge is no longer functional.)

We knew and enjoyed the lake from West End all the way to its eastern shore at Little Woods where we sometimes fished and crabbed from the porch of a friend's weekend camp. One of our favorite family outings was a Sunday afternoon ride along the lakeshore. Many years later I enjoyed taking my father for drives along the same route, our roles reversed from the time in my childhood when he did the driving to entertain me and my brothers and sister. We'd start out at West End and follow the winding shore to the New Orleans Airport where we'd spent some time watching planes take off and land, a pleasant, simple way to spend a morning or afternoon. I think that drive along Lake Pontchartrain was one of the scenic delights of the city.

Lake Pontchartrain afforded recreational opportunities all year round and obviously was very much a part of our lives.

Ironically, we seldom saw or were even aware of that body of water the city is so famous for—the Mighty Mississippi.

The Mississippi

Our house on Prytania Street was less than a mile from the Mississippi. Yet, for all we saw of it the river might have been a thousand miles away. Although the port was New Orleans' major industry, the river that supported it was virtually invisible. Hidden by a wall of warehouses and wharves, it was, to the city at large, an unseen presence whose voice was the sound of foghorns in the night. There were, however, occasional rents in the wall. In the absence of a river bridge, most of these rents were landings for the ferryboats that plied the river, carrying passengers from shore to shore. Ferries ran back and forth between Canal Street and Algiers, Jackson Avenue and Gretna, Louisiana Avenue and Harvey, and in our general neighborhood, between Napoleon Avenue and Marrero and Walnut Street and Westwego. All of these westbank destinations were small towns except for Algiers which, although separated from the city by a half mile of water, was actually a part of it.

My introduction to the river was by way of the Napoleon Avenue Ferry, when one day, with Mother in the front seat and Brother and me in the back, Daddy drove the short distance from our house to the ferry landing at the foot of Napoleon Avenue. There, at the top of the road that climbed the levee, I first saw the Mississippi. This first encounter came as a great surprise. I could hardly believe that the quiet stream the foghorns conjured up for me was in reality this huge, ferocious, yet majestic river. Although the ferryboat was tied up at the dock, I hardly noticed it. Instead, I stared unblinking at the river's muddy water as we drove onto the ferry's deck. As soon as Daddy parked the car, its front bumper almost touching the deck's railing, there was a loud frightening explosion which, it turned out, was the ferry's whistle. Then, in tandem with the low growl of the engine, the ferry shuddered, lurched forward and we were on our way.

As it chugged towards the far shore, buffeted by the current, I too was buffetted, but by anxiety. My chief worry was the awful possibility of the car breaking through the railing and plunging into the river. Yet, perversely, I refused to leave the car, for who was to say that I, myself, wouldn't fall in. By the time we reached the west bank, however, Daddy had somehow convinced me that all was well. Since we were tourists, if only temporarily, bent on seeing the river itself, we didn't disembark at Marrero, but stayed aboard for the return trip. This, I later learned, was an old New Orleans custom. Indeed, New Orleanians had long since used the ferries as excursion boats as well as means of transportation. As a result, many New Orleanians knew very little about the small towns across the river. Even, Algiers, technically a part of the city, could well have been as far away as the Algiers in North Africa.

On our way back to the city, Mother and Daddy coaxed Brother and me, or rather coaxed me, for Brother was raring to go, out of the car to take a look at the river from the ferryboat's upper deck. From this windswept eyrie, the domain of the ferry's foot passengers, we had a broad panoramic view of blue skies, drifting clouds and rushing, chocolate-colored water. Seagulls dipped and wheeled above us, tree trunks hurtled past us in the swirling current, and tugboats towing gravel-laden barges chugged by in slow motion. As we approached the shore, Daddy pointed out the ferry landing, the public cotton warehouses, the dark red brick, almost Dickensian, buildings of the Lane Cotton Mills and the lovely slim spire of St. Stephen's Church on Napoleon Avenue.

This, our first ferry ride, was only the beginning. Through the years, Mother and Daddy treated us to many such excursions, juggling ports of embarkation so that we could see the waterfront in its entirety. It was from the Canal Street ferry, coming back from Algiers, that we had our best view of the city. Seen thus from the river, the contrast between New Orleans' original French colonial settlement and its American offshoot was at its most compelling. To our left, the modern skyscrapers of the Business District soared and, to our right, the spires of the St. Louis Cathedral rose above the Vieux Carré. During the week before Mardi Gras we sometimes saw a giant grey battleship, all of its flags flying, or came upon the harbor's fire tug in the midst of a demonstration. This tugboat, actually a nautical fire engine, was designed to fight the fires that occasionally flared on ships or on the docks. It was an exciting experience to watch this small boat pumping water from the river and shooting it in towering geysers up into the sky.

As we rode the ferries, we eventually became accustomed to the sight of dry docks, teeming wharves, feverish dockside activity and all manner of ships and boats. But of all the ships and boats, our favorites were the great ocean-going vessels, especially those that flew the flags of far away, exotic lands. In time, we learned to identify their flags and to distinguish between cargo and passenger ships and also between different steamship lines. All of this, of course, was from afar. One day, however, we had the unexpected pleasure of boarding a French ship. A friend of Mother's who was going to spend a month in her native France invited Mother and Daddy, Brother and me to the ship to see her off. This was a great thrill for all of us. It was also my first opportunity to air the French I had been studying for the five long years since I was four. Upon telling Daddy that I was thirsty and would like a glass of water, he gallantly escorted me about the ship until we found a steward. Face to face, however, with this suave Frenchman, I lost my nerve and, with it, my French vocabulary. Indeed, it was only by resorting to sign language that I was able to make myself understood. My thirst was there-fore slaked, but my ego, unfortunately, was not.

There was an open stretch of water at the back of Audubon Park where the Mississippi was plainly visible from the levee. It was there that Daddy took us in the springtime to see the swollen river which, following its North-ern thaw, sometimes rose to an alarming height. Always awesome, the Mis-sissippi could be terrifying at this time of the year. Plummeting headlong towards the Gulf of Mexico, it was quite capable of sweeping across the bat-ture---the flat, low-lying land on the riverside of the levee---submerging the trunks of its willow trees and coming precariously close to the top of the levee itself. Happily, Daddy allayed any fears we may have felt at this raw display of nature before we reached the river. Each year, he reminded us that, despite its height and ferocity, the river would not overflow. This, he said, was because of the Bonnet Carré Spillway, a huge diversionary project thirty miles upriver from the city which would be opened in the event of danger-ously high water. In that case, he explained, 250,000 cubic feet of water per second, a mind-boggling surge twice that of Niagara Falls, would pour into the spillway and eventually, by way of Lake Pontchartrain, reach the Gulf. Daddy assured us that this magnificent engineering feat made flooding of the city virtually impossible. Armed with this guarantee from one who was, him-self, an engineer, we were able to watch the river with a feeling of confidence that bordered on exhilaration. Indeed, the only fear we felt was for the ships that sailed, as if on stilts, above our heads, for they were in peril of the up-rooted trees and other flotsam that were tossed about like matchsticks by the current.

Occasionally we drove up the Avenue towards the bend of the river where St. Charles and Carrollton Avenues meet. Upon arriving there I was always delighted and, somehow, rather surprised to see the levee so close at hand. Forming a backdrop to the threshhold of Carrollton Avenue, the grass levee with the green plumes of the batture willow trees rising up behind it, imbued the area with a fresh country atmosphere and the promise of wide-open spaces nearby. Sometimes Daddy parked the car and suggested that we climb the levee for a look at the picturesque colony of driftwood houses that covered the batture. The batture was not privately owned, but was considered to be a part of the river and belonged to the United States government. Free, there-fore, of rent and city taxes, it was a promised land for squatters. Although a shanty town, the small community didn't seem to be a slum. As a protection against spring flooding, its houses were built on pilings or on flatboats. Most of them were surrounded by small gardens and extended by porches that af-forded a magnificent river view. Their occupants fished, gathered driftwood, tended their gardens and kept pigs and chickens. They also sold wicker furni-ture which they made from the batture's willow trees and, after a good catch, peddled fish and river shrimp. One spring, Daddy took us to the foot of Car-rollton Avenue to show us how the batture dwellers coped with the high water. We saw at once that they had coped magnificently. Although water covered the foundation pilings of their homes and swished just beneath their porches, which, at that point, teemed with frightened pigs and chickens, dogs and cats, the houses themselves were high and dry. So were the houseboats which, having popped up like corks with the water, were cheek by jowl with the stilt houses nestled under their umbrella of willow trees.

As we grew older, Mother and Daddy sometimes took us for a harbor tour on the steamboat *President*. This huge sidewheeler, 298 feet long with a capacity for 3,000 passengers, was a beauty. Her hull was steel, but her gleaming white superstructure was made of wood. From each of her five decks--- and Brother and I had a glorious time running up the stairs between them--- there was a far more comprehensive view of the river and the port than there was from any of the ferryboats. For the *President*, unlike the ferries, cruised parallel to the shore, upstream and downstream, past miles of harbor views. Her upstream destination was Six Mile Point which was six miles from her berth at Canal Street and almost to the upper boundary of Audubon Park. This turning point provided me with one of my biggest thrills aboard, that of seeing Audubon Park from the river instead of seeing the river from Audubon Park. Much of the fun we had on the *President*, however, had nothing to do with the view. We were happy as larks when putting nickels in the coke, candy, or bubble gum machines or, best of all, trying our luck at the Iron Claw. But although we invariably landed a pocketful of the claw's trinkets, we never did succeed in maneuvering it to clutch the Mickey Mouse watch we coveted. I, for one, loved the *President*'s dance floor. Brother could take it or leave it, but I was fascinated by its gigantic mirror-smooth expanse. Indeed, I had a wonderful time imagining how it would look at night when it was packed with dancers swaying to the music of a big name band.

Although the river view had strong competition on the *President*, it had absolutely none from the summit of the Huey P. Long Bridge. It was always a thrill to drive across this soaring bridge that spanned the Mississippi at Nine Mile Point in neighboring Jefferson Parish (County). The bridge, at the top of its span, was as high as a 36 story building, and the view it offered was, therefore, a magnificent perspective of the distant skyline of New Orleans and miles of verdant flatlands gracefully threaded by the river. From our vantage point it was clear that the Crescent City had extended far beyond its original boundaries. Indeed, it had extended so far it was embraced by double crescents or, as Brother insisted, a giant letter S.

Catching the Brass Ring - City Park

All children experience certain thrills growing up, thrills that later in life remain strong and poignant memories. I experienced some of my first childhood thrills in City Park. City Park was where I climbed my first oak tree, took my first dive off the high diving board, caught my first brass ring on the flying horses, and rode a pony for the first time; it was where I learned to swim, paddle a canoe, and play tennis; it was where I went skating and bikeriding and picnicking.

City Park was the major entertainment center for me and the other children in our neighborhood. Besides all the activities I've mentioned, we enjoyed concert and dance recitals at the City Park Bandstand, visits to Delgado Museum, football games at City Park Stadium and hayrides to Spanish Fort. As teenagers, we sipped sodas and munched hot dogs and popcorn while we socialized at the Big Casino in the park.

For city children the park was nature's school, teaching us our first lessons in botany and zoology, although we didn't realize it at the time. Learning about acorns and oak trees, mud divers and locusts, butterflies and caterpillars, perch nests and bird calls was just part of the fun of the park. The park was where we took our pet ducks, flying squirrels and turtles when they got too big to handle at home. We set them free, confident that they would like their new home and hopeful that we would see them again from time to time on our frequent trips to the park.

The park grounds we became so familiar with had been farm land and cow-grazing pastures in French colonial times. The original 85 acres of park property was owned by French colonist François Héry, who received title

135

to the land in 1718, the year of the city's founding. This land eventually became the plantation of the Allard family and it is that name that is associated with the park tract. A marker on City Park Avenue and a short street nearby named Allard Boulevard recognize the Allard ownership. This land was on the outskirts of town when the park was first opened in the late 1850s and visitors spent a full day making the round trip to the park from the city by horse-drawn carriage.

After a long period of neglect following the Civil War the park had a rebirth in 1891 when a coalition of downtown politicians and business leaders organized the City Park Improvement Association. This Association, now the City Park Board, spearheaded the park's revival and developed it into today's 1,500 acres of natural and man made beauty.

As a child I enjoyed the park just as it blossomed into the full flowering of its modern beautification and expansion. During the 1930s the Works Progress Administration, with millions of dollars of federal money, conducted extensive improvements in the park (just as it did on the lakefront). Over 20,000 men and women worked on the park, embellishing and rejuvenating the landscaping, building bridges, lagoons, and fountains, erecting statues, creating golf courses and ball fields. They also built City Park Stadium (now called Tad Gormley Stadium) and the Art Deco adorned Rose Garden.

One of my first recollections of the park was an excursion there with my father. Benny, Helen, and I played under the giant oak trees on City Park Avenue and stuffed our pockets full of acorns, which we later roasted at home (I didn't like the way they tasted but they were lots of fun to collect). We climbed on the low hanging branches of the great McDonogh Oak named for philanthropist John McDonogh, without whom there may not have been a City Park. McDonogh acquired the Allard Plantation in 1845 and bequeathed it to the city when he died in 1850. My father told us that McDonogh had been a recluse and had a scary reputation during his lifetime. "Children and dogs used to run away at the sight of him," my father said. Despite this, McDonogh's philanthropy provided both recreation and education for thousands of New Orleans children, including us. (His money funded the public school system as well as the park.)

There were lots of other oak trees to climb on besides the McDonogh Oak. Our favorite was the Suicide Oak by the swimming pool. Its serpentine branches spread out in all directions almost hugging the ground. They bobbed up and down like hobby horses when we straddled them, but sometimes there were so many of us climbing the branches, sitting on them, hugging them and hanging from them that they became grounded and motionless from the weight of us all.

When we were little we called all of the oaks "dueling oaks." It sounded romantic and adventurous. "At one time there were so many duels in City Park," my father used to tell us, "that men had to wait in line to get shot at." When one of the real Dueling Oaks died and was uprooted in 1949, years after our tree climbing excursions, workmen found a pair of gold pince nez and two bowie knives under the roots.

Climbing the oaks was often combined with feeding the ducks, an amusement my father enjoyed almost as much as we did. He told us how to tell the difference between the male and female French ducks (the males are much prettier) and warned us to stay away from the geese. "Geese can be mean," he said. That was easy to believe since they always approached us aggressively honking and hissing. The really dangerous birds I decided, however, were the black swans. I still love the way they look but I have steered clear of black swans ever since the day one chased me, trying to grab a piece of bread out of my hand, and ripped the skirt loose from my dress. Years later when I saw "Swan Lake" with the villanious Odile I thought "Oh, boy, that librettist really knows black swans."

Encounters with other park creatures were more amiable and sometimes unpredictable. Like my first adventure with mud divers and locusts. One of Benny's favorite things to do in summer was to hunt along the park's Museum Mall for mud divers. These were crusty looking bugs that hid in holes with mud chimneys and miraculously turned into beautiful flying locusts. We called them locusts, but just like mosquito hawks, that was not their real name. When I was in high school biology class I discovered that they are really cicadas and the mud divers are the pupae, the third stage in their life cycle. In their adult stage the males "sing" an annoying piercing song that sounds something like a knife grinding machine. Anyway, when I was about 10, Benny showed me how to capture mud divers by pouring water down their holes; they come to the surface to avoid drowning and you pop them in a bottle or just put them in your pocket if you're not squeamish. Benny would place the divers on the screens of our back porch and watch their metamorphosis, much like watching a butterfly emerge from its chrysalis. When the adult locust appeared, leaving an empty mud-diver's shell behind, Benny would carefully pick the locust from the screen and set it free on a tree outside where its wings would dry and it would fly away.

On my first solo mud-diving expedition, I returned home with several large mud divers and unbeknownst to Mother I placed them on a screen inside the house. Having a short attention span, I forgot all about them. That night our family went out to a movie. When we returned, our house was filled with flying locusts, shrieking their heads off as they zoomed from room to room. That was the last of my mud-diving expeditions to City Park for quite some time.

Once in a while on a Sunday, after an hour of canoeing or rowing around the park's lagoons, my father took us to Delgado Museum. I got to know the paintings by heart, nothing ever seemed to change there. My favorite painting for a long time was Bouguereau's "Whisperings of Love." I considered the lady of the painting the most beautiful creature I'd ever seen. Another painting I always looked for was the one with the cardinals in their brilliant red robes, Jehan Vibert's "The Cardinals' Friendly Chat." Both paintings still hang in the museum and when I see them I always experience a nostalgic twinge of *déjà vu*.

Even as a child I was impressed with the Museum's beautiful setting, at the end of tree-lined Lelong Avenue. It's easy to see why philanthropist Isaac Delgado designated that site when he decided to give the city $150,000 for a museum building. I always thought the museum one of City Park's special attractions. In recent years it has greatly expanded and become a nationally recognized art center and is not so specifically identified with the park. It is no longer known as Delgado Museum but the New Orleans Museum of Art. However, the original 1911 museum building still bears Delgado's name.

Just a short distance from the museum over the lagoon bridge in the direction of Bayou St. John was an imposing structure which seemed to be in the park, but was actually a private estate belonging to oil millionaire William Harding McFadden. We referred to it as "the McFadden place" and sometimes strolled past its elaborate gardens trying to catch a glimpse of life inside that storybook setting. All we ever saw was an occasional gardener or caretaker. The seven-bedroom, eleven-bath mansion was built in 1920 and had a large marble-lined indoor swimming pool as well as a trophy room, ballroom, library and several drawing rooms. Its grounds included an oriental garden, a sunken garden, a lovers' lane, a stable, dog kennels, greenhouse, and caretaker's lodge. City Park acquired the mansion and its four-acre site in 1943 for $40,000. It is now leased to the Christian Brothers School.

A visit to City Park was never complete without a stop at the Big Casino, the sprawling Spanish-mission style building behind and to the left of the museum on Dreyfous Drive. It was always crowded and noisy; a friendly, high-spirited kind of noise, the happy noise of people having a good time. The aroma of popcorn and hot dogs filled the air. Soda jerks were busy serving up sodas, sundaes and double-decker ice cream cones. There was a claw machine in one corner and Benny often talked my father into letting him play. He tried all kinds of maneuvers with the crane-like gripper to retrieve something from the treasures and trinkets jumbled together on the floor of the machine. Once, with my father's help, he managed to extricate a wristwatch which was buried under a mass of worthless objects. However, it didn't work.

When I was older and went to the park on skating and bike-riding expeditions or on school picnics, the Casino was the gathering place for boys and girls to get acquainted, do a little flirting and sometimes have a first date.

Right outside the Casino was the Bandstand, a raised platform with Ionic columns topped by a bronze dome. Besides the Sunday afternoon concerts (directed by Professor Michael Cupero) that we attended, the Bandstand was the setting for small dancing-school recitals and talent shows. Helen, the dancer of our family, appeared twice in recitals at the Bandstand, much to the amusement of Benny and his friends. Even more amusing, I'm sure, were the impromptu singing and dancing we all engaged in when the Bandstand was unoccupied by scheduled and bona-fide performers.

Nearby was the beautiful and imposing Peristyle, which we called the Lion Pavilion. It looked like a classic Greek temple with Ionic columns all around it. It had been built in 1907 as an outdoor ballroom dancing pavilion and it had a wonderfully smooth surface. It made a perfect skating rink. On brisk fall or winter days we skated to City Park and spent hours at the Pavilion, going through what we considered intricate maneuvers. We sometimes imagined ourselves on ice floating gracefully around like Sonja Henie. We had to be awfully careful not to float right out into the lagoon, for the Peristyle was positioned on the banks of the lagoon with steps leading down to the water. Two majestic lions flanked the stairway, hence "Lion Pavilion."

Some of my fondest recollections of City Park are associated with the swimming pool and flying horses (carousel). From the time I was six years old until I was about twelve, we went swimming at the City Park pool four or five times a week during the summer months. Mother had decided that swimming was not just for fun, it was good for us. It was a lucky day for us when she talked to a doctor who extolled the salubrious benefits of swimming. Not to go at anything half-heartedly, she saw to it that we had maximum exposure to the healthful waters of City Park Natatorium.

And we did not just go there, take a quick dip, and return home. No, we traveled to the park as an expeditionary force. For one think, we *walked*--- at least two miles from our home on Gentilly Boulevard. That also was *good* for us. But surprisingly, the journey was also fun---almost as much fun as swimming and riding the flying horses. We always took with us assorted neighborhood children, as many as seven or eight. My mother brought along the customary supply of sandwiches, cookies and a big thermos of juice or root beer. We each had our own little bundle, consisting of towel, bathing suit and bathing cap (for the girls). We started off about 8:30 a. m. and whatever friends wanted to go with us showed up by that time--they knew our schedule.

We marched along Esplanade Avenue in the shade of huge oak trees. As we neared Moss Street and Bayou St. John I always ran ahead to catch a glimpse of that breath-taking vista across Esplanade and the bayou down Lelong Avenue to the graceful, imposing outline of Delgado Museum. This picture postcard view contrasted sharply with the crowded, bustling, noisy scene on the banks of the bayou. At that time the bayou was crowded with houseboats and pleasure boats moored at the shore or anchored just off shore. There were lots of people coming and going, some fishing or crabbing from the bridge, some hanging out wash on their houseboats, others negotiating the gangplanks loaded with bags of groceries. We waved to those who looked our way and exchanged pleasantries with the fishermen: "Are they biting today?" "What kind of bait are you using?" "Is your hamper full of crabs?" Occasionally we'd happen by as someone hooked a giant garfish and we'd stay to watch him land it. I remember one garfish that looked about ten feet long. Benny said the bayou was full of gars and the fishermen hated them because the gars ate so many of the good fish there weren't enough left over for the fishermen.

Benny made friends with several of the houseboat people because he fished so often at the bayou. When he was twelve years old my father gave him a skiff and he kept it tied up to one of the houseboats. The old couple who lived on it often invited him in for sandwiches and cookies. I always thought it would be fun to live on the water as those folks did and I felt sorry for the boat people when they had to leave their bayou homes. The summer after they left, the waterway seemed empty and dull without them. In the late thirties the City Park Board evicted all houseboats between the Esplanade Bridge and the Black Bridge (the railroad bridge towards the lake) and by 1948 the waterway was cleared of all remaining boathouses and wharves between the Black Bridge and the lake.

Nowadays it's hard to envisage the bayou as the busy, commercial waterway it once was, filled with barges carrying construction supplies and produce to the city. At one time there was a drawbridge at the old Indian portage (near Bell Street) and it cost $1.00 to pass the bridge and enter the "port" of Bayou St. John. Commerce increased with the building in 1795 of the Carondelet Canal from the bayou's headwaters to the center of the city at Basin Street between Toulouse and St. Peter Streets. The canal's turning basin was where the Municipal Auditorium now stands. Commercial activity declined during the early 1900s and the bayou filled up with boathouses, shipyards and houseboats. The Carondelet Canal was filled in between 1927 and 1938 and almost all of the bayou came under the jurisdiction of the City Park Board in 1934. It was gradually transformed in the ensuing years to the peaceful waterfront park it is today.

After we crossed the bayou at Esplanade we rounded Beauregard Circle at the entrance to the park, taking time for a quick inspection of the equestrian statue of General P. G. T. Beauregard, erected in 1915. This fiery Creole gentleman, my mother told us, started the Civil War by firing the first shot at Fort Sumter and he was the last general to surrender, after General Grant and General Lee met at Appomatox Courthouse.

Past Beauregard's statue the quiet lagoons and greenery of the park enveloped us and we quickly completed the trek down the mall, around the museum, past the tennis courts and playing fields and finally to the swimming pool.

We paid our twenty-five cents admission and went through the turnstile to the bath house, another of the park's mission-style structures with a red-tile roof. After getting into our suits, we headed for the pool; but first we had to negotiate a passageway spouting water from all sides and then step into a medicinal footbath at the end of the passage, the sanitary precautions of the day. "Last one in's a rotten egg," we shouted as we raced to be the first in the pool.

That first summer we started going, Benny and I took swimming lessons from a Red Cross instructor who gave us a badge and certificate when we finished the course. We spent most of our time, however, on the diving boards.

There were three boards, two one-meter boards, and one three-meter board. The "hell-diver," as we called the three-meter board, was the pool's major attraction. Kids lined up ten deep to take their turn jumping or diving from its height. At the age of six the "hell-diver" looked as tall as a four-story building. With the encouragement of my favorite lifeguard (my first serious crush) I harnessed enough courage one day to climb up the ladder and walk out on the board. One look down at the water and I retreated to climb down the ladder. This went on for several days until I finally took the plunge. By this time all the regulars at the pool had been keeping up with my climbs up and down the ladder and I received a rousing cheer as I emerged from that first dive. That was all I needed. I spent the rest of the morning, indeed the rest of the summer, diving from the "hell-diver."

The other big attraction of the pool was a raft anchored in the middle. Swimming out to it was the test of our swimming capability and self-confidence. The first time we did it we felt we were real swimmers, whether we had that Red Cross badge or not. When we felt like taking a breather, we parked ourselves on one of the stone cascades at either end of the pool.

Mother kept a watchful eye on all these activities from a bench just outside the fence surrounding the pool, always looking cool under her parasol. There was a big clock on the wall behind the high diving board and when it said 12 o'clock that was our signal to get out and get dressed.

(The swimming pool, I am sorry to say, no longer exists. It had been one of the park's most popular attractions from the time of its opening in 1925, the gift of philanthropist William Ratcliffe Irby, until the early 1950s. After closing in 1958 the pool successively became a seal pool, a monkey pen and a miniature golf course. Today it is unused and sadly overgrown with hedges and weeds.)

After our exuberant hours in the pool followed by lunch and playing on the drooping limbs of Suicide Oak, we had barely enough energy for the trip home. Spirits were always high when we started out in the morning, with us running, hopping and skipping on ahead of Mother. The return trip was in reverse, with Mother plugging ahead and the rest of us straggling out behind her. We got our second wind when we passed St. Louis Cemetery Number 3 on Esplanade Avenue and ran in there for a quick game of hide and seek.

On Mondays when the pool was closed, Mother sometimes took us to the park for a picnic. The picnic grounds, across the street from the pool on Victory Drive, were shaded with huge oaks and had scads of swings, slides, and see-saws. To cool off we waded in the Hyams wading pool and fountain. After lunch we headed for our favorite park amusement---the flying horses.

I loved everything about the flying horses: the painted steeds studded with colored stones, the whirling ride flashing our reflections in the mirrored walls, the camaraderie of being with friends, the lilting strains of the music, and most of all, the thrill of catching the brass ring. There was a certain mystique about the brass ring. It wasn't just that you got a free ride if you caught it; there was a special feeling of satisfaction and pride if yours were the lucky fingers that snatched the last ring as it thunked into place just barely within your reach; and of course, you were the envy of your companions. There was a unique timing and rhythm to the flying horses. First, there was just enough time between rides to jump on and select your steed, always an outside flyer (the kind that moves up and down). We felt certain horses were particularly lucky. Mine was a blue charger with yellow jewelled eyes and lots of red stones on his body. Then, as soon as we were on our steeds, the music started and we began moving slowly around, gradually picking up speed until we were whirling at an exciting clip. Next, the buzzer went off, signalling the extension of the metal arm bearing the rings. One by one the riders plucked off the worthless steel rings. Excitement mounted as time drew near for the last ring, the bright brass ring to drop into place. It was a matter of luck. Would you be in the right spot at the right time? And a matter of dexterity and strength. Could you lean over at just the right angle and snatch hard enough to dislodge the ring? The first summer I didn't catch any rings at all. But the following year I managed to pluck quite a few loose, including a brass ring. I caught my share in the years that followed but no matter how many I caught I never lost the thrill of that first lucky catch. The flying horses are still in City Park, housed in the same 1906 building where I spent so many hours trying to catch the brass ring.

Many New Orleanians share my fond memories of City Park. Often I've heard people say "I grew up in City Park" as they recall their years of swimming, picnicking, boating, biking, climbing trees, playing ball, and riding the flying horses.

Besides our regularly scheduled round of activities in the park, we also attended special events there; like the time in 1937 when President Franklin Roosevelt dedicated the Mall named in his honor and when the Catholic Church celebrated the Eighth National Eucharistic Congress in City Park Stadium in 1938.

The park even played a part in our Mardi Gras celebration, for it was where the Mid-City parade lined up to begin its procession on the Sunday before Mardi Gras. The park was our favorite spot when we rode in the truck parade on Mardi Gras during our high-school and college years. Following the Rex parade our trucks would head for City Park for an afternoon of eating and ball playing.

Mardi Gras

Ask a child in any part of the United States to name his favorite holiday and he'll probably answer "Christmas". Unless he lives in New Orleans. If he does, he'll probably answer, "Mardi Gras."

I don't remember how old I was when I realized that everyone in the world did not celebrate Mardi Gras. I do remember how shocked I was and how I pitied all the children who had no Mardi Gras in their lives. It just didn't seem fair. One September I consoled a new girl in school who missed her hometown of Elkhart, Indiana, by telling her how lucky she was to live in New Orleans because she could take part in Mardi Gras. Long before Mardi Gras arrived---in February that year---she had decided that New Orleans was more fun than Elkhart anyway; Mardi Gras was icing on her cake.

For a New Orleanian, Mardi Gras has a magic that spans generations, classes, and political and religious differences. No matter how many parades I have seen and no matter how reluctantly I go to still another one, once I hear the crowds and smell the popcorn and cotton candy my heart beats faster, my feet start to skip and excitement stirs my spirit. Those vestiges of my childhood have never left me.

Excitement and anticipation were the essence of our childhood celebrations. Christmas, birthday parties, Easter egg hunts and summer picnics all kept us awake the night before. They gave us exhilarating peaks in the plateaus of our lives. The excitement and anticipation of Mardi Gras were greater than those of any other holiday, maybe because Mardi Gras let us indulge our passion for make-believe. Our generation grew up listening to "Let's Pretend" on the radio and thrilling to the swashbuckling adventures of Errol

145

Flynn, Tyrone Power, and Clark Gable at the movies. Mardi Gras gave us the opportunity to live out our fantasies, at least for one day.

That one day of Mardi Gras (French for Fat Tuesday) is the climax of the whole Carnival season, which officially begins twelve days after Christmas on Twelfth Night (January 6). Twelfth Night ushers in a round of Carnival balls, the highlight of the New Orleans social season.

During my childhood I was not aware of the balls and supper dances, of the social whirl that centers about the kings and queens, the maids and courts of Carnival. In my family and neighborhood we celebrated the Carnival season with rounds of King Cake parties that lasted from Twelfth Night to the Sunday before Mardi Gras. Carnival lasts from four to nine weeks depending on the date of Mardi Gras, which is dependant on the date of Ash Wednesday, which is dependant on the date of Easter, which is dependant on the full moon that follows the spring equinox. During that time we concerned ourselves with what we were going "to be" for Mardi Gras. Hardly a day went by that children didn't ask each other, "What are you going to be?" We considered masking a major part of our Mardi Gras fun. Sometimes we knew exactly what we wanted to be and repeated our roles from year to year, wearing a different costume, of course. I was a gypsy at least three times. But sometimes we agonized for weeks over our Mardi Gras persona until Mother finally gave us a deadline. She made our costumes and needed time for her preparations. Helen usually chose girlish, storybook characters like Little Bo-Peep, the Littlest Rebel (Shirley Temple in pantaloons), or Sleeping Beauty. I usually chose adventurous characters. If I wasn't a gypsy, I was either a pirate or an Indian.

In my childhood, the festivities before Mardi Gras Day telescoped into six days of revelry, beginning with the first parade on the Thursday before Mardi Gras. The Knights of Momus paraded and we loved them! They danced and twirled on their floats, blowing kisses and kicking up their heels, all the while holding on to their support poles, keeping their grotesque masks in place and throwing beads and trinkets to the crowd.

Since Mardi Gras usually comes in February, a month of bad weather in New Orleans, we must have endured some cold and rainy parade nights, but the weather never dampened our enthusiasm or dimmed the brilliance of the passing pageantry. All the parades from my childhood form one memory of thumping drums, blazing flambeaux, glittering floats bearing masked riders in fantastic costumes and thousands of people jumping up and down, waving and shouting "Throw me something, Mister."

Our parade-going fervor never wavered even though we walked to and from the parade route, a distance of about three miles each way. From our house on Gentilly we walked to Esplanade Avenue, out Esplanade to Dauphine Street and up Dauphine to Canal Street. We always walked with two or three other families, all shepherded by our mothers; I don't remember that any of our fathers ever came along. We talked, joked and sang along the way. We walked faster as we neared Canal Street and ran ahead to listen for the low rumbling that always preceded a parade. The crowd on Canal Street usually lined the curb five or six deep. We tried to worm our way to the front so that we could look down the street to catch our first glimpse of the approaching floats. When the sky began to glow and we heard the faint whine of police motorcycles, we shouted, "It's coming, it's coming," and began to jump up and down and wave as though the floats were already passing. We jockeyed for position on the front row, but pushed back to the curb as the motorcycles drove by, brushing perilously close to us. We pushed farther back as the mounted police passed, guiding their horses right up to the crowd to widen a path for the parade. My mother clutched us to her side, but after the horses passed we squirmed free and ran back into the street. Finally we saw a police car and the parade krewe's repair truck. Beyond them, we saw a tiny halo of light. As it grew, we saw the king on his throne, waving his scepter and bowing to his subjects. We waved and shouted at his mule-drawn float drew near, but we reserved our most exuberant demonstrations for the floats that followed (except for the title float which had no riders). We leaped into the air trying to catch strings of beads or trinkets.

I tried as hard as anyone else to catch the attention of the maskers on the floats, but my favorite characters in the parade were the captain of the krewe and his dukes. Resplendent in robes of gold, silver and brilliant colors, they wore plumed helmets and velvet capes draped over the backs of their horses. They waved their riding crops at the crowd and bowed their heads in greeting as the crowd applauded them. I watched them with quiet and almost reverential admiration. For me they embodied the romance and mystery of Mardi Gras. I experienced one of the greatest thrills of my childhood when a duke beckoned me over, reached down, patted my head and pressed a tissue-wrapped package into my hand. It contained the most beautiful string of pearls I had ever seen (so I thought at the time). I treasured it for several years and wore it for dress-up occasions when I was in high school.

I didn't have much success in snagging "throws" as they sailed through the air, but Benny always caught more than he wanted and shared his catch with Helen and me. I was interested only in the glass beads. Some of them looked as pretty as costume jewelry. On our way home from the parades we compared our loot with that of our friends. I often traded handfuls of whistles, horns, rubber balls, yo-yos and combs for one pretty string of beads.

Our trip home from the first Carnival parade was always an anti-climax. But our spirits lifted as we looked ahead to the Hermes parade the next night, to Mid-City on Sunday, Proteus on Monday night and finally Rex and Comus on Mardi Gras.

The only parade I didn't enjoy was the Children's Parade, held on the Saturday afternoon before Mardi Gras. It definitely lacked the pomp and circumstance of the other "real" parades. The Krewe of NOR (New Orleans Romance) which included children from New Orleans public and parochial schools, sponsored the Children's Parade. The krewe chose its king and queen from honor students whose names were submitted by the schools that belonged to NOR. Students, parents and teachers designed and decorated the floats. This sounds like a good idea but my own lukewarm reaction to the Krewe of NOR must have reflected a general view because it quietly disappeared from the Mardi Gras scene after World War II.

When I was in the sixth grade I marched with the St. Rose de Lima school band (I attended St. Rose that year) in the NOR parade. I played the snare drum, an instrument I took up shortly before the Carnival season began that year and which I gave up shortly after it ended. Since that parade, I have had profound respect for the members of marching bands. Never have I ever felt so tired and frustrated as I did during that parade. I had done a lot of walking in my life, but never in rhythm while trying to beat a drum, keep a uniform cap on straight and maintain my dignity amid noisy, jostling crowds. I had always been sorry to see a parade end, but not that one.

The parades of Mid-City on Sunday and Proteus on Monday night completed our warm-up for Mardi Gras Day. Our family celebrated Mardi Gras the same way for many years. We started the day with coffee and doughnuts, the traditional Mardi Gras breakfast. Only on Mardi Gras Day my mother cooked the doughnuts herself, frying them and dusting them with powdered sugar as soon as she snatched them from the pot of hot oil. We packed any doughnuts left on the platter after breakfast along with our picnic lunch. By one or two o'clock in the afternoon they had become soggy and heavy as lead but we ate them with gusto. For lunch my mother packed sandwiches with *panné* meat, lots of apples and bananas, and cocunut cake for dessert. We always prayed for good weather because we didn't want to cover our costumes with coats and sweaters. For Helen and me, dressing in costume had the added thrill of putting on make-up. We applied liberal amounts of lipstick, rouge and eyebrow pencil, a ritual we were permitted on only one other day of the year---the day of the annual dance review. Donning our costumes took a bit of doing. We always had problems getting oilcloth boots in place (for the pirate costume), keeping pantaloons up, or tying the gypsy headpiece at a suitably rakish angle. When we felt satisfied with the results we added the final touch, our thin black satin masks. We wore our masks almost continually until the Rex parade ended, for we considered them an essential part of our masquerade.

When we had finished dressing we burst out the front door and down the front steps and stopped. We immediately sensed something different about the day. Excitement pervaded our neighborhood. Like an electric charge, it flew from us to our friends who joined us as we hopped, skipped and jumped on our colorful trek to Canal Street and the Rex parade. Other maskers emerged from their homes along the way to form a throng charging up Esplanade Avenue.

At North Claiborne we met a band of "Indians," one of the groups of Negroes who dressed elaborately in feathers and beads, and danced, leaped and whooped up and down the streets of their "territory." The Indians had established themselves in Mardi Gras tradition and we always looked for them on our way to Canal Street. New Orleanians of mixed Negro and Indian blood organized the first "tribes" in the 1880's. The Indians' popularity grew and soon tribes flourished all over the city. There were the Wild Tchoupitoulas, the Golden Blades, Yellow Pocahontas, the Creole Wild West and many others. We heard tales of how competing tribes fought over their territories, resulting in occasional stabbings and shootings, but we only saw the Indians in celebration, stomping their feet and leaping in warpath dances, chanting and whooping and marching around proudly displaying their spectacular regalia. They wore costumes of unmatched extravagance, with elaborate and intricate designs of beadwork trimmed with crystals, spangles, sequins, rhinestones and fur. They wore feathered headdresses, some of which fanned out like mantles and flowed to the ground. Our maid Beulah told us that some costumes cost thousands of dollars and took all year to make. Her uncle belonged to the "Black Eagles" and she said that as soon as one Mardi Gras ended he started to make his tribal regalia for the following year.

By the time we reached North Rampart Street, crowds of people were milling about and occasional short parades of musicians and marching clubs filled the streets. Everyone wore costumes. We saw clowns, bunnies, apes, ballet dancers, minstrels, artists, devils, angels and other traditional masquerades. The maskers who impressed me most were those who completely covered themselves with odd things like playing cards, Coca-Cola bottle tops, buttons, or brass bells. Occasionally we saw maskers striding on stilts, towering above us and somehow keeping their balance in the bustling crowd. I particularly remember a man dressed in an authentic-looking Uncle Sam costume. On stilts and wearing a top hat, he looked twelve feet tall. The smell of cotton candy, peanuts and popcorn filled the air.

We proceeded to Dauphine Street and then up to Canal Street where we took up residence on the neutral ground with thousands of other paradegoers to await the arrival of Rex. That wait always seemed endless, although moments of excitement and entertainment interrupted it frequently as marching clubs or impromptu walking groups strutted by, cavorting and capering about. Occasionally our group joined hands to form a chain. We wove our way up and down the block, laughing and doing a little cavorting of our own.

One year I remember feeling a great stir of excitement in the crowd and I thought the Rex parade was coming; but instead we saw King Zulu and his followers, who had wandered off course. I felt disappointed because Zulu's floats and riders looked so raggedy and threw only coconuts. I had no idea that some years later I would spend most of Mardi Gras morning searching for the Zulu parade and would have gladly traded all of my beads for one coconut. The Zulus, a Negro Carnival club organized in 1909, had little appeal for me in my childhood when I yearned for the glitter and glamour, the baubles and beads of the traditional Mardi Gras parades. But when I grew older I didn't consider my Mardi Gras complete until I saw King Zulu, the Witch Doctor, the Big Shot of Africa and all the other free-wheeling Zulus whose parade perfectly parodied the Rex parade.

At least once when Rex still provided the highlight of my Mardi Gras celebration, I stood close enough to the Boston Club to see clearly the King of Carnival toasting his Queen, ensconced in her flag-draped stand in front of the Boston Club. Earlier in the day we had admired her and her maids, dressed in lovely pastel suits with hats to match and wearing orchid corsages. After they had drunk toasts to each other, the king threw his glass to the ground. Soon his float lumbered onward and we scrambled to catch some throws as the rest of the parade passed by. We greatly resented the riders throwing most of their favors to the people in the Boston Club stand, however, and we made it a point never to watch the parade in that spot again.

After our days of anticipation, the Rex parade ended all too soon. I considered the trucks that followed an unglamorous and disappointing denouement to Rex. (Today's elaborate truck parades are a popular addition to Rex). We consoled ourselves with food as soon as the last float had passed. Munching sandwiches and cake, we strolled up and down Canal Street, inspected the department store windows filled with mannequins in elaborate Carnival costumes and jewels, and tried to talk my mother into letting us stay uptown until time for the Comus parade. Occasionally she gave in and took us to a movie at the Saenger or Loew's State to pass the time. After a couple of hours of rest and entertainment in the dark theater, we went out for our final Carnival fling. We moved to Royal Street so that we could enjoy the brilliance of Comus' floats as they passed through the narrow, dimly lit French Quarter, and could see up close the antics of the strutting, whiterobed Negroes bearing flares and flambeaux, the gasoline torches used to illuminate the shimmering, brightly colored floats.

When the last float went by and the crowd began to disperse, we wearily walked homeward. Our spirits sank. Our costumes, so fresh and shiny as we started out that morning, looked as dreary as our moods. No matter how many strings of beads we had caught, no matter how many sights we had seen, we could not forget tomorrow. We had lost our identities as gypsies and pirates, princesses and devils; we were only school children headed back to the classroom and the real world.

My experience of Mardi Gras was different in many ways from Margaret's. Her chapter on Carnival gives you a glimpse into the world of Carnival balls and supper dances, a facet of the season's festive celebration that is perhaps more typically "uptown" than "downtown."

Carnival

Soon after Christmas, Carnival was upon us; for the evening of January 6, or Twelfth Night, marked the traditional opening of the ball season leading up to Mardi Gras. All of a sudden, Mother and Daddy were glamorous creatures going to balls and Brother and I were busy planning our costumes for Mardi Gras Day. But long before that day arrived, we were treated to a glimpse of Carnival as seen through adult eyes.

One morning the parlor, deserted when the Christmas tree came down, sprang to life again and we realized with a tingle of excitement that Mother and Daddy were giving a party before a ball. The parlor's sliding doors yawned wide, a fire crackled in the grate and a bowl of iris, daffodils and ferns—carrying out the Carnival colors of purple, green, and gold—adorned the mantel. Delicious odors wafted from the kitchen, the vacuum cleaner hummed and the doorbell rang all day. One of the deliveries always gave me a thrill, for it fulfilled my youthful ideas of sophistication and romance. A gift from Daddy to Mother, it was a purple orchid nestled on a bed of cellophane in a glistening see-through box.

When the party began, Brother and I, ready for bed in our pajamas and robes, were perched on the stairs peeping through the banisters. As the guests arrived, the entrance hall was a swirl of icy air, excited greetings and luxurious wraps. Then, when everyone moved into the parlor, the party became a scene right out of fairyland. Firelight suffused the room. It painted rainbow hues on ballgowns, struck flashing sparks from jewels and made faces and bare shoulders rosy. In the glow of this illumination, all the women were beautiful and all the men were handsome. But to us, Mother, with her fair skin, sapphire eyes and softly waved brown hair drawn back into a little knot, was the most beautiful of all. And Daddy, blond and boyish in his tails, was the handsomest. No matter how much they were enjoying themselves, they never failed to notice us in our eyrie on the stairs. Now and then, Daddy winked and pulled a funny face to make us laugh and Mother waved and blew a kiss.

The party was always of short duration because everyone wanted to get to the ball on time. I longed to go with them to see the king and queen, the maids and dukes, the all-powerful captain, his lieutenants and the members of the krewe. I also longed to be "called out" to dance with a masker and receive a favor from his satin bag. But, alas, no fairy godmother came to grant my wish. Instead, when the guests began to leave, Mary, our nurse, whisked us off to bed.

But when I was nine years old, a fairy godmother materialized in the person of my uncle who was the captain of a ball---the ball, however, shall be nameless for the position of the captain was top secret. Having each year withstood my pleas to see the ball, my uncle suddenly and unaccountably capitulated. His invitation, however, was limited. I was to see the tableau and the grand march, but only backstage from the wings, and leave before the "call-outs" began. Brother, to his indignation, was invited too. Although just five, he thought of himself as a rugged he-man and stamping his foot, announced he wouldn't go. Yet go he did and, to his surprise, enjoyed himself immensely.

As soon as we entered the stage door of the Municipal Auditorium where the Carnival balls were held, we were engulfed by swarms of spirited maskers. But instead of feeling the elation I anticipated, I felt a surge of fear. The grinning wax masks, some of them grotesque, scared me half to death and I clung to Daddy like a limpet. Brother, however, didn't turn a hair, but fraternized with the maskers as if he were a member of their krewe.

Before long, the shrill blast of a whistle caused a hush to fall upon the room. Looking up, I saw a shining being dressed in cloth of gold, high white leather boots and a plumed silver helmet. With a thrill of recognition, I realized that this shining being was my uncle. Still unmasked and grinning broadly, he gave a smart salute and signalled Daddy to take us to the stage wings.

Once there, I could hardly contain my excitement. On a crimson carpeted dais I saw two gleaming golden thrones and, all around them, my favorite characters from the nursery rhymes. They were painted on the scenery, molded into giant *papier mâché* figures and incorporated into the columns that formed a semicircle behind the thrones. Near us, the grandfather clock of Hickory Dickory Dock towered above Old King Cole, his pipe, his bowl, and his fiddlers three, and across the stage Little Miss Muffet sat on her tuffet beneath an evil-looking spider and Little Jack Horner pulled a plum from his pie. While I stared, wide-eyed, at these *papier mâché* marvels, Brother focused on the stage hands who were scurrying about making last minute adjustments to the lights and scenery. There was a flurry of activity when the king strode onto the stage followed by eight velvet clad dukes who took their places on either side of the dais while he walked up the steps to his throne. Then, suddenly, the captain's whistle blew. And when it did, the band struck up, the curtain rose and the ball began.

Gorgeously attired lieutenants led the krewe members as they gleefully erupted into the room. After a few minutes of prancing about, the entire krewe sat down on the ballroom floor, forming a huge semicircle. Then the maids were led out one-by-one by swallow-tailed committeemen. Gowned in white and carrying dainty nosegays, they approached the stage amid the appreciative cheers and whistles of the krewe. After each maid curtsied to the king and joined her duke beside the dais, the great moment of the ball arrived.

Trumpets blared, the ball guests rose and the young queen, escorted by the captain, appeared upon the ballroom floor. Shimmering like moonlight in her sparkling gown and jewels, she was the embodiment of every princess in all the fairytales I'd ever read. Hand in hand with the captain, her velvet mantle fanning out behind her, she seemed to glide across the floor. As she approached the dais, the captain stopped, leaned down and whispered in her ear. Bewildered, she hesitated for a moment, then, turning, looked straight at me and smiled. Once again, I felt a thrill of recognition. I knew the queen! My fairy princess had become, as if by magic, real. She was my mother's godchild, Katherine.

As I watched, transfixed, she ascended the red carpeted steps of the dais and took her place beside the king. When they were seated, the Pied Piper, in bright yellow and spring green, bounded onto the stage and piped a merry tune. In his wake came Mother Goose, Little Boy Blue, a cow, a sheep, four dancing ears of corn, the Old Woman in the Shoe and her numerous progeny. They all cavorted in a lively skit, then quitted the stage in a comic conga line. The king and queen acknowledged these antics with a wave of their scepters, then led the maids and the dukes in a triumphal grand march around the ball-room floor.

When they returned to the stage, Daddy told us it was time to go. "But first," he said, "look across the ballroom floor and see who's in the middle box." We looked, and there was Mother! As if by a prearranged signal, Daddy nudged us forward and whispered "Wave." To our surprise, Mother saw us, waved back and blew a kiss. With this delightful encounter, our big evening came to an end. Daddy took us home. Then, returning to the ball, he escorted Mother to the supper dance.

On parade nights, only Momus, Comus and Proteus in those days, Brother and I were keyed up to a fever pitch. After an early dinner, Daddy drove us to the Garden District to see the parade on St. Charles Avenue. Although he parked as close to the avenue as possible, we were usually three or four blocks away. This meant a brisk and chilly walk in a milling crowd along the time-worn brick sidewalks of the neighborhood. As we plunged headlong towards the avenue, I could sense the pent up excitement of the crowd, an excitement that would soon erupt at the parade. My own excitement was intensified by the Garden District's beauty and its old-world charm. Lining the sidewalks were large gardens enclosed by lacy ironwork fences and lux-uriantly planted with boxwood, azaleas, camellias and sweet olive, crepe myrtle and banana trees. Towering above them were ancient live oaks and magnolias and antebellum mansions that loomed mysteriously in the darkness. For me, these heirlooms of a bygone age rivalled the glamour of the parade and created a romantic aura that I still associate with Mardi Gras.

As we approached the avenue, we smelled the heady aroma of peanuts, popcorn, cotton candy and hot dogs drifting from the stands of street vendors. Daddy always bought us a treat, usually hot roasted peanuts, to keep us happy until the parade came. Before long we saw a pink glow breaking through the treetops. Then we heard the tattoo of motorcycles and the blare of bands. We felt a quiver of excitement. The parade was coming! Brother and I could hardly wait to see the glittering floats, the mule teams that pulled them and the gyrating, white robed flambeaux carriers who lighted their way. But we were mainly interested in catching the beads and trinkets that the maskers threw. Screaming "Throw me something, Mister!" at the top of our lungs, we were occasionally showered with a rain of "throws." This happened when a masker recognized Daddy, his head above the crowd and one of us perched on his shoulder.

The night my uncle rode--another uncle this time--we were afraid he wouldn't find us. Yet he always did. For each year we stood at the same place on the parade route and he and his fellow riders were on the lookout for us there. When they spotted us, shouting and waving frantically, they pelted us with "throws." Then came the magic moment we were waiting for. My uncle waved us to the float, leaned over the side and handed each one of us a bulging bag of beads.

On Mardi Gras morning, Brother and I popped out of bed like jacks-in-the-box, eager to put on our costumes. Brother was usually a cowboy or an Indian, but I always chose a costume that was feminine and pretty. I loved to be an old-fashioned girl, for then I could preen in a long, panniered gown set off by rouged cheeks and a black *mouche*, or beauty spot, accenting my bright, painted lips. After a Mardi Gras breakfast of doughnuts and milk, we dashed to the porch to watch the crowds of maskers streaming towards the Garden District to see the Rex parade. Tall rabbits holding sleepy little bunnies, Raggedy Anns and Andys, big scary gorillas, Little Red Riding Hoods and scores of other animals and storybook characters passed before our dancing eyes. Occasionally a small marching band decked out in satin and plumes strutted by playing Dixieland. This raucous syncopation whipped the crowd into a frenzy of clapping and dancing. Trucks decorated according to a theme and filled with matching maskers inched along, honking at the pedestrians to clear the road. We could always expect to see truckloads of clowns, gypsies, hobos, hula dancers, artists and pirates. Some of the trucks boasted small combos and when halted by the traffic, their passengers jumped out and danced in the street. The delirium mounted as the crowd swelled and, finally, it was time for us to leave for the parade.

Most of the families who lived along the parade route on the avenue had open house on Mardi Gras day, inviting friends and relatives to watch the parade from their porches and front lawns. We were lucky, for we received an invitation every year. For Brother and me this meant a grand view of the parade, a party, lots of playmates and a sense of freedom that would have been impossible in the crowds. There was a tacit agreement that we children could run about as we pleased as long as we stayed within the boundaries of the tall wrought iron fence. Until the parade came, we played in the yard, blissfully unaware that adult eyes were watching out for us.

Although every child wore a costume, none of the grownups did. It was apparently *de rigueur* for them to dress both formally and in the latest fashion.

Indeed, some of the women rushed the season by wearing flowery spring hats.

At the first sign of the parade, most of the men came into the yard to offer a shoulder to a child. This perch, coupled with a slight elevation of the lawn, gave us a clear view of Rex, the King of Carnival, and his colorful entourage. The lumbering *papier mâché* floats made a magnificent show with their fluttering decorations of flora and fauna and their glittering gold leaf which, especially on a sunny day, was dazzling to behold. We always caught a lot of "throws," for some of the maskers spotted friends in the yard and threw them an avalanche of beads.

When the parade had passed, along with the small procession of decorated trucks that followed in its wake, we all went inside for lunch. The dining room table, decorated with flowers in the Carnival colors, groaned beneath platters of ham, roast beef and fried chicken, bowls of potato salad and steaming tureens of red beans and rice. We children were served on paper plates which, in fine weather, we carried outside for a picnic on the lawn, while the adults balanced fine china on the porch. In the afternoon we ran races, played games and traded "throws" until it was time to go home. At this point, Brother and I were always so tired and sleepy that we left without a murmur. Sometimes, in fact, we were so tired that we fell asleep in the car and, still sleeping, were carried inside and tucked into bed in our costumes. When we awoke the next morning, it was to a completely different world, a world in which fasting displaced feasting. Mardi Gras, like Prospero's banquet, had vanished into thin air. It was Ash Wednesday, the first of forty days of Lent.

The War Years

Mardi Gras, along with many other New Orleans celebrations, vanished for several years when World War II interrupted the provincial, static life of the city and things were never the same again. The war years were a transition between one era and another.

Soon after Pearl Harbor the city began to take on a military aspect. Our lives were gradually directed or controlled by the exigencies of wartime living. Because of New Orleans' importance as a port and its strategic location near the mouth of the Mississippi and the Gulf of Mexico, it was a prime military center. Shipbuilding became a major industry and Army and Navy installations mushroomed up and around town bringing an influx of servicemen to the area.

The war meant rationing and black-outs, war bond drives, patriotic projects, and of all things---lady bus drivers and streetcar conductors. The grim realities of the time hit home when relatives or friends were drafted or joined the armed forces and when rumors pervaded the city of Nazi submarines lurking at the mouth of the river.

My personal reaction to the war---I was a sophomore in high school at the time of Pearl Harbor---was one of shock and disbelief. Once that wore off I found the war exciting, almost exhilarating. We had so many war time projects at school that life was filled with exciting and important things to do. All that propaganda about the war effort found receptive young minds and hearts at McDonogh High School. It wasn't until my brother Benny, a student at Tulane University, joined the Navy's V-12 program and was sent overseas that I fully comprehended the horrible possibilities of war and lived with the gnawing anxiety and fear of all families who had loved ones in the armed forces.

Meanwhile I was active in the War Relief Club at school. All club members had uniforms---tan khaki with gold buttons---and we worked like beavers to "further the cause of victory." We wrote letters to servicemen, we knitted socks and sweaters under the supervision of a Red Cross volunteer, we sold War Savings stamps, we raised money by collecting tin foil, old clothes, wire coat hangers and old auto license plates. We participated in patriotic parades and rolled bandages at Charity Hospital. We had a Books for Boys group that sent books and magazines to servicemen all over the country and overseas. In the space of two years time we supplied the boys with over 2,000 items of reading material. We suffered burn-out on that particular project and abandoned it to turn our efforts to planting victory gardens. The object was to sell our produce at a year-end auction and use the money to buy a hospital bed for our allies, the British.

I had been an avid and successful participant in all of the War Relief Club activities but the victory garden proved my undoing. My assignment was cabbages. My mother would not relinquish any of her flower garden space for my project, but a kind neighbor allowed me the use of an arid and rocky plot in his back yard. I attacked it vigorously, made some small dents in the packed earth, neatly etched some rows and optimistically planted my seeds. To my delight they sprouted and for a few weeks I took pride in watching them grow and branch out. Each week at our club meeting members described the progress for their carrots and turnips and parsley and I told how famously my cabbages were doing. Then something terrible happened. The little plants just quit growing. I watered them, pulled up the weeds that constantly threatened to engulf them, and gave them my utmost care. One day holes began to appear in the leaves and before I knew it the entire crop was wiped out.

Each week the other gardeners, however, continued to describe the success they were having with *their* crops. My own reports became less enthusiastic, but quite short of straightforward honesty. Harvest time and auction time approached. I faced each day with a sense of dread and finally devised a painful scheme to save face. The day of the auction I took several months' savings from my allowance---five dollars---and went to the Le Breton Market. I was amazed at how expensive cabbages were. I had thought to buy at least a dozen, that would have been respectable, but I only had purchasing power for nine. Miss Minnie Belden Stanley, the teacher-advisor of the War Relief Club, conducted the auction. She remarked on the cleanliness of my cabbages---they had no traces of soil or sand as did the rather scraggly looking specimens the other gardeners brought in. To my chagrin, my beautiful cabbages that I had painfully forked over $5.00 for brought in a mere $3.00. It's a good thing the war effort didn't depend on victory gardens for success.

In our family life the war made an almost immediate impact with the onset of rationing, practice blackouts, and a general lifestyle that provided fewer luxuries than even the Depression years. Because of the vital importance of the port and the numerous Army and Navy installations in the city, New Orleans was considered a possible bombing target and we had periodic blackouts and air raid practices. My mother made shades for our windows with blackout cloth and my father became an air raid warden. He wore a metal hat and carried a flashlight as he made his rounds of the neighborhood every time the siren went off signalling a blackout. He sometimes returned home disgruntled because some of the neighbors had less than adequate blackout provisions. He told us how it was possible for enemy airplanes to spot a target just by the light of a single match. We made sure that not a millimeter of light escaped from *our* house. I remember what a thrill it was the first blackout when we went outside and looked up at the sky. No enemy airplanes were in sight, but rather the starry panorama of the heavens, brightly and startlingly visible as they had never been before. This inspiring sight prompted us to embark on a study of astronomy. My father bought us a telescope and every blackout we would enjoy the heavens not just for their beauty but for the fun of finding the Pleides, Ursa Major and Minor, Leo, Cassiopeia, Pegasus, Perseus and other constellations.

Of course, we never experienced the horrors of real bombing raids---except vicariously through the newsreels and movies like "Mrs. Miniver" and "Waterloo Bridge"---but the immediacy of the war overseas came home to us with the arrival at school of a wartime refugee. Elizabeth Steele from Glasgow, Scotland was sent by her parents to stay with friends in New Orleans for the duration of the war and joined our class at McDonogh High School. She was an instant celebrity and captivated all of us with her Scottish brogue, bright blue eyes and ebullient manner. The *Times-Picayune* newspaper featured an illustrated story about her and all of us at school basked for a time in her limelight. Elizabeth gave periodic reports at school assemblies on news from home and how her family was faring through the uncertainties of life in Britain during the war. She was the darling of our class and when she had to return to Scotland after the war, scores of tearful teenagers showed up at the Southern Railway Station on Canal Street to bid her a sad farewell.

Although we knew that life in the United States during wartime was luxurious compared to life in Great Britain we had a hard time adjusting to things like rationing. At first the idea of tightening the belt for the war effort was inspiring. I tackled the job of mixing the food coloring into oleo-margarine with a patriotic fervor. I endured "meatless Tuesdays" with cheerful fortitude. I learned how to repair my bicycle tires and did so ad infinitum. After a while the deprivation of meat and butter and rubber and other non-essential commodities became irksome. I talked my mother into saving some ration stamps for a once-a-month splurge to buy whipped cream which I beat into butter and then doled out sparingly to make it last as long as possible. Despite all the latest health reports on the invidious effects of butter consumption and the improvement in the quality of margarine, I am still a butter freak and margarine still tastes like yellow lard.

My father found wrestling with rationing more frustrating even than I. My mother assigned him the task of shopping for meat. Because of limited supplies, customers would line up at the LeBreton Market early in the morning before the meat stalls opened. Although my father was often first in line he seldom "brought home the bacon" because, chivalrous soul that he was, he allowed himself to be elbowed aside by the more aggressive housewives in the line. He would return home discouraged and dispirited. My mother finally took over this duty and our menus improved immediately.

Patriotic slogans and messages in the movies and over the radio picked up our spirits and war bond drives spearheaded by movie stars spurred our support of the war effort. Every teenage girl in town must have showed up at the Municipal Auditorium---judging by the crowd and the squeals---the night Errol Flynn appeared on the stage to sell war bonds.

New Orleans had Army and Navy hospitals located along the lakefront and one of our teachers--an especially patriotic soul--conceived the idea of staging a variety show for the entertainment of "the boys" there. She conducted a talent hunt among her students and for some unknown reason I wound up in the final cut. Out little troupe included an acrobat, a tap dancer, several singers and an accordion player. Our master of ceremonies was a neighborhood boy, A. G. Kleinschmidt, Jr., who was actually very funny and very talented. I, unbelievably, played the piano and sang "Into the Wild Blue Yonder." Poor boys, they must have realized even more forcefully after our performance that "war is hell."

These reminiscences of the war are for the most part light-hearted but our primary feelings were ones of fear and anxiety, especially as we saw friends and relatives leaving home to serve their country. Newsreels of actual combat and reports of casualties intensified these feelings. In my own family, no one breathed easy until Benny returned home from Okinawa after the war was over.

The War Years

Unlike Elsie, we were spared the anxiety of having someone in our family overseas. My youngest uncle, whose warmth and wit were sorely missed, left his law practice to serve in the army, but he remained in the states throughout the war. Although Brother longed to go into the service, the war was over just a month after his eighteenth birthday. In any case, a childhood polio attack, though mild, would have prevented him from going.

Following Pearl Harbor, we--like everyone else---were immediately plunged into a new way of life. Its impact was dramatically felt in our neighborhood. Just a few blocks from our house--at the downtown lake corner of Valence and St. Charles---was a turn of the century mansion that served as the Japanese Consulate. On Pearl Harbor Sunday, the Japanese in their haste to destory confidential papers, made a bonfire of them on the lawn. The sight of this conflagration brought the reality of the war home to me more vividly than anything else that happened that day.

It was just a matter of time before air-raid practice began. Our sitting room was designated as a "shelter" and mother lined its drapes with black material so that we could keep the lights on when the sirens blew. We were thus able to settle down to our usual evening pursuits. We all knew, however, that there were German submarines in the Gulf and---practice raid or not-- I, for one, was always glad to hear the all clear sound.

Rationing came as a surprise, but soon turned into a humdrum, everyday affair. Rosie had a hard time making do in the kitchen, for meat was rationed as were sugar, coffee and butter. I can still hear her muttering about the Japanese and Germans as she mixed a bowlful of white lardlike oleomarga-

rine---a food that was entirely new to me---with bright yellow food coloring.
"It ain't natural", was Rosie's dictum about this yellow substance that took
the place of butter for the duration. Pies, cakes and ice cream became all
but obsolete for want of sugar. And coffee---also in short supply---was sweet-
ened with saccharine tablets. But Rosie, ever a magician in the kitchen, worked
wonders throughout the war. I especially remember her magic touch with
Spam---that most maligned of wartime staples. Her baked Spam was good,
her Spam au gratin better, and her Spam à la king was delicious. Shoes also
were rationed and silk stockings were virtually non-existent, as were the nylons
that had come on the market just before the war. We painted our legs, however,
with tan leg makeup that was fine as long as the weather held but ran when we
were caught in the rain.

Sunday drives in the country and cruises on the boat soon became things
of the past, for gasoline and tires were rationed too. But if we could have
driven out along the River Road we would have seen something new, for, since
the beginning of the war, Camp Plauché had sprung up on land near the Huey P.
Long Bridge.   The lake front had also undergone a change. It was transformed
by military installations that stretched eastward from the New Basin Canal
to Shushan Airport. Occasionally Brother and I drove out to the lake with
Daddy to spend the afternoon on the boat. But we couldn't take her out,
for she was tied up in her slip for the duration. While Daddy and Brother
checked the engine, pumped out the bilges, polished brass and touched up
the paint, I stretched out on the deck to get a suntan. Sometimes we drove in
the direction of the Yacht Club to take a look at the Coast Guard Station
just across the New Basin Canal and the U. S. Army Hospital---Camp Lagarde---
situated at its rear. Unseen by us, there was another hospital---the U. S. Naval
Hospital---on the far side of Camp Lagarde and, beyond it, another Coast Guard
Station and other military areas including a German Prisoner of War Camp.
One day in another part of town I saw some of the German prisoners, all
of whom seemed very young and very blond, being transferred to the camp
in an army vehicle. Upon seeing me---a girl as young and blond as they were---
they broke into spontaneous smiles and waves. It was a strange sensation
to experience this friendly greeting from the enemy, and flustered, I lowered
my eyes until their truck moved on.

As Elsie said, there was no Mardi Gras during the war years. Two days
after Pearl Harbor, the following proclamation was issued:

"WHEREAS, war has cast its gloom over our happy homes and care usurped the place where joy is wont to hold its sway.

"Now, therefore, do we, deeply sympathize with the general anxiety, deem it proper to withold our Annual Carnival Festivity in this goodly city, and by this Proclamation, do command no assembly of the

Rex Organization

Parade or Ball

February 17th, 1942"

That Mardi Gras night of February 17th, however, a magnificant Army and Navy Relief Ball was held. The Municipal Auditorium was packed with guests who had contributed to the war effort in order to attend the ball. The courts---or queen and maids---of several Carnival balls of former years were among the ball's participants. As it happened, I was a maid in a court---Osiris ---of the current, cancelled season that also took part in the ball. I therefore had the fun, not to mention the excitement, of participating.

A Hollywood luminary often spearheaded events that were held on behalf of the war effort. The Army and Navy Relief Ball was no exception. Ann Rutherford, a young actress who played Mickey Rooney's sweetheart in the Andy Hardy movies and also one of Scarlett's sisters in Gone With the Wind, was chosen as the Queen. I remember being in transports at the rehearsal, for not only were Miss Rutherford and I introduced, but we carried on a conversation. I could hardly believe that I was, at long last, meeting a real, live movie star!

Several days after the ball, a friend hailed me on the Newcomb campus--- I was a student at Newcomb College at the time--with the startling information that she had seen me in the newsreel at the Saenger. I quickly rounded up a couple of cronies and, in a flash, we were on the St. Charles streetcar on our way downtown. It was a big thrill for me to see myself on the Saenger's big screen---scared to death but proud as a peacock---as I promenaded around the ballroom floor.

To contribute to the war effort, I wrote letters to my uncle, a cousin and friends in the service, rolled bandages at the Convent---which was then my alma mater---and saved a portion of my allowance to buy war stamps. I also knitted sweaters which, I'm afraid, fell far short of my expectations--- not to mention, I imagine, the expectations of the boys who received them.

Every Sunday afternoon, Rebelles---an organization to which I, and many of my friends belonged---sponsored a tea dance for officers in the Fountain Lounge of the Roosevelt Hotel, now the Fairmont. Our mothers took turns acting as chaperones, and although they didn't dance with the officers, seemed to enjoy themselves thoroughly.

The Officers Town House downtown also sponsored dances that many of us attended. I suppose it could be said that we boosted the officers' morale by going to Rebelles and the Town House. But, as it turned out, the officers boosted our morale too. For as the war continued, there were very few boys who were near our age still at home.

Sometimes it seemed as if the war would never end. But, at long last, in August 1945, the Japanese surrendered and we were at peace. On V. J. night, a large group of us---all girls and all jubilant---went downtown to celebrate. The crowds on Canal Street were ecstatic. To a counterpoint of horns, whistles and pealing churchbells, the people in the crowds laughed, cried, sang and exchanged exuberant greetings. Churchhill's V for victory sign was given over and over again, soldiers and sailors embraced pretty girls and were, in turn, embraced and total strangers hugged and kissed as if they had known each other forever. It was a night I'll never forget! I remember wondering on the way home if there would ever be another war. But, considering the atomic bomb, I didn't see how such a thing was possible.

Epilogue - New Orleans Today

It is obvious that growing up in New Orleans in the '30s and '40s, whether uptown or downtown, was a lot different from growing up in the city these days. And although we look back with affection and some nostalgia on the culture and customs that we come from, we think there's a lot to be said for growing up in New Orleans today. Who would want to live without air-conditioning, for one thing. In fact, we think New Orleanians today have the best of both worlds, a culture and ambience that is still unique in the United States and conveniences and opportunities undreamed of before World War II.

It was following World War II that we experienced so many astonishing changes in the city. It's only by looking back now from the present perspective that we realize how great those changes were. A wave of construction and modernization took place throughout the city, suburbs sprang up overnight, the pace and mobility of life quickened dramatically, and in a relatively short space of time the city seemed to take on a new image. This is starkly evident in the skyline, still changing almost daily with the addition of more skyscrapers.

Although we've had the Huey P. Long Bridge over the river since 1935, it was the building of the Greater New Orleans Mississippi River Bridge in 1958 spanning the river at the Central Business District that spurred development of the West Bank of the river. The 24-mile long Causeway over Lake Pontchartrain, reputedly the world's longest bridge, enabled many New Orleanians to combine the enjoyment of country living on the north shore of the lake with the cultural, recreational, and vocational advantages of the city. An influx of Cubans and Vietnamese added even more variety to the city's already diverse melting-pot of French, Spanish, Negroes, Germans, Irish, English, Italians, Haitians, Greeks and Yugoslavs.

It's no longer rare to meet someone who is not a native New Orleanian. In fact it's quite usual. The extension of the city to the east and over the river has added a new and somewhat strange dimension to life in the Crescent City. It is possible for newcomers to New Orleans to settle in one of these outlying suburbs and never experience New Orleans at all. We've met women who have moved here from Ohio and Michigan, live in New Orleans East, work in New Orleans East, shop at the Plaza in Lake Forest (in New Orleans East) and think New Orleans is no different from Cleveland or Detroit. We hope that most newcomers will take the time to experience the French Quarter, the Garden District, the Riverfront and Lakefront and all the places and events that make New Orleans special.

Today's New Orleans offers an even greater melange of treats for its citizens and visitors than ever before. While some of the holidays and holy days we talked about are not observed with the same fervor of our growing-up years, we have other celebrations like the Jazz and Heritage Festival that have added a whole new dimension to the city's roster of entertainment events. This egalitarian celebration of music, food and crafts has captivated our children, ourselves, and a wide spectrum of other New Orleanians as well as visitors from all over the state and country. The once elite Carnival subculture has broken out of its aristocratic bounds, and it is now possible for almost all New Orleanians to participate in a Carnival krewe or parade if they so desire. In fact Mardi Gras mania has spilled over into outlying sections. Besides the enormous Carnival activity in adjoining Jefferson Parish, there are parades and balls in Covington and other communities across the lake and as far away as Pass Christian, Mississippi.

A great feature of today's New Orleans is the river---so remote to us as children and now so much a part of our cultural and recreational scene. Canal Place at the foot of Canal Street, the Moonwalk across from Jackson Square, the Riverview and boat dock at Audubon Park Zoo are all part of this development. Perhaps the greatest legacy of the 1984 World's Fair will be the further expansion of the Riverfront for all New Orleanians to know and enjoy.

Other advantages our children have experienced because of the emergence of a more vigorous and cosmopolitan New Orleans are a nationally recognized New Orleans Museum of Art, the Contemporary Arts Center, fine ballet and opera companies, an internationally recognized symphony orchestra, the Louisiana Nature Center in New Orleans East, a nationally acclaimed Audubon Park Zoo, a wide variety of art galleries all over the city, a revitalized French Quarter, the Superdome, and many other cultural and recreational facilities unknown in our growing up years.

Of course an important change in the fabric of New Orleans society since we were children has occurred in the area of race relations. We grew up in the era of "screens" on buses and separate water fountains and rest rooms. It was the way things were when we grew up and you can get a pretty good idea of racial roles in reading our reminiscenses. The fact that today the city has a black mayor and four black council members as well as blacks represented in almost all other areas of the city's political, cultural, educational and recreational life tells how that situation has changed.

Tourism, a word seldom heard when we were growing up, has now become a major part of the New Orleans economy and has helped shape much of the city's recent development.

The preservation movement has come, belatedly but now effectively, to prevent the destruction and distortion of much of the city's architectural and cultural heritage. And with preservation has come a renewed interest and pride in our neighborhoods. Following a small exodus of New Orleanians to the suburbs some years ago, there has been a return to the city, especially on the part of young professionals.

Is there still a big distinction between uptown and downtown? You bet there is. Some sections of the Faubourgs Marigny, Trémé and New Marigny and other areas of downtown are undergoing extensive restoration and residents there are becoming more aware of their neighborhoods' history and heritage. In the uptown area, some run-down sections of the Lower Garden District and Irish Channel as well as Uptown's modest neighborhoods on the far, or river, side of Magazine Street are being transformed into fashionable, desirable and expensive pieces of real estate. The Garden District is still elitist and beautiful and Uptown remains a "silk stocking" enclave whose mystique is as strong as ever.

Some people still worry, like architect Benjamin Latrobe did so long ago, that New Orleans may lose its distinctive flavor and become like any other American city. To that we say: our children may not have experienced the New Orleans we did, but they can still ride a streetcar, go to Mardi Gras parades, feast on oyster poorboys and gumbo, watch ocean-going ships on the river, listen to jazz on Bourbon Street, enjoy coffee and doughnuts at the French Market, fish for game fish within the city limits, roam the French Quarter, and sail on Lake Pontchartrain. Nowadays they can even ride a gondola a-cross the Mississippi. And we think our children's children will be doing the same thing. New Orleans become just like any other American city? Not on your life!

SELECTED BIBLIOGRAPHY

Bordes, John Paul, *John-Paul Sez, Columns on Carrollton.*

Cable, Mary, *Lost New Orleans.*

Carter, Hodding, ed., *The Past as Prelude: New Orleans 1718-1969.*

Chase, John Churchill, *Frenchmen, Desire, Good Children.*

Christovich, Mary Louise, *New Orleans Interiors.*

Costa, Louis; Neff, André; Raarup, Peter, *Streetcar Guide to Uptown New Orleans.*

Dufour, Charles L., *If Ever I Cease to Love.*

Federal Writers' Project of the Works Progress Administration for the City of New Orleans, *New Orleans City Guide.*

Freiberg, Edna B., *Bayou St. John in Colonial Louisiana, 1699-1803.*

Friends of the Cabildo, *New Orleans Architecture* Volumes I, IV, V & VI.

Garvey, Joan B. and Widmer, Mary Lou, *Beautiful Crescent.*

Griffin, Thomas K., *The Pelican Guide to New Orleans.*

Hennick, Louis C. and Charlton, E. Harper, *The Streetcars of New Orleans.*

Huber, Leonard V., *New Orleans, A Pictorial History.*

Huber, Leonard V. and Wilson, Samuel, Jr., *The Basilica on Jackson Square.*

Huber, Leonard V., *Mardi Gras: A Pictorial History of Carnival in New Orleans.*

Kane, Harnett T., *Queen New Orleans, City by the River.*

Kirk, Susan Lauxman and Smith, Helen Michel, *The Architecture of St. Charles Avenue.*

New Orleans Chapter of the American Institute of Architects, *A Guide to New Orleans Architecture.*

Preservation Resource Center, Holiday Home Tour. *Guide Book to Rose Park, Everett Place and Richmond Place.*

Reeves, William and Sally, *Historic City Park.*

Rivet, Hilton L., S. J., *The History of the Immaculate Conception Church in New Orleans.*

Samuel, Martha Ann Brett and Samuel, Ray, *The Great Days of the Garden District and the Old City of Lafayette.*

Tallant, Robert, *Mardi Gras.*

The Original Picayune Creole Cook Book. Eleventh Edition.